COLORADO PLATEAU

Enjoying the
SOUTHWEST

*An Unusual Guide to One of America's
Last Remaining Frontiers of Unspoiled
Natural Beauty. With Notes on Its
Geology, Archaeology, Anthropology, and
History, plus Practical Advice on How
to Plan an Exciting and Satisfying Trip*

Enjoying the SOUTHWEST

by

Catryna Ten Eyck Seymour

Drawings by the Author

J. B. LIPPINCOTT COMPANY

Philadelphia and New York

U.S. Library of Congress Cataloging in Publication Data

Seymour, Catryna Ten Eyck, birth date
    Enjoying the Southwest.
    1. Southwest, New—Description and travel—1951–
—Guide-books. I. Title.
F787.S49   917.9′04′3   73–4617
ISBN–0–397–00902–X
ISBN–0–397–01008–7 (pbk.)

To
Polly
Thaddeus
Liz
T.
Sam
Mary Duffie
Abigail
and
Aljo
who made it all possible

Contents

Preface

I was seventeen years old when I first saw the Southwest. My family took me there on what was to be a traditional sight-seeing trip until I was left for several days with my great-aunt, Leslie Van Ness Denman of San Francisco, who had taken an active interest in the Indian arts of the Southwest. She took me to Second Mesa, where we witnessed the Hopi Snake Dance, and to Canyon de Chelly, where we went into the canyon and saw the cornfields and pastures worked out of the desert by the Navajo Indians who have made their home in the canyon for centuries. The trip made a deep impression on me, particularly my visits to the Indian country.

A generation later, when my husband and I and our own teen-age children discussed a family trip to the Southwest, I recalled the visits to Second Mesa and Canyon de Chelly and urged that our itinerary include those places. In searching for material on which to base the planning of our trip, however, we discovered that information about these and other areas was sparse, and many months were consumed in corresponding with various state offices, Federal agencies, chambers of commerce, and other sources for literature about the Southwest. When we had collected all that was available, we sorted it out in piles according to the different states and slowly but surely developed a travel plan. What resulted was an exploration of the Southwestern United States that was every bit as exciting as a trip to a foreign country and which avoided crowds and tourist trappings.

Our trip to the Southwest in the summer of 1971 also introduced us to the pleasures of camping—not rugged mountain climbing and sleeping in pup tents or lean-tos, but camping in the comparative comfort of a small travel trailer (which we borrowed from my husband's brother, Thaddeus Seymour). We are a city-raised family, used to the comforts of modern urban living, and the discovery that living out of doors can be comfortable and delightful was a special bonus added to the trip.

When we saw the grandeur of the natural scenery which has been the concern of the Sierra Club, the Wilderness Society, and other conservation groups and realized for ourselves that this was still a great unspoiled frontier, we decided to prepare this guidebook in hopes that it may aid in building a constituency of informed and sympathetic people who would help ensure the protection and preservation of the area. You will see that the book is not designed to attract the casual tourist who is looking for gaudy and ephemeral pleasures. They can be found elsewhere. This book is directed rather to those thoughtful citizens who find excitement in the history of the pioneers, in the beauties of nature still relatively untouched by man, and in the fascination of the different worlds of the Indian and other inhabitants of this remarkable land.

Neither is this guide designed to be a definitive portrayal of the Southwest. It does not cover the cities, except for brief mention in the final chapter. It does not include a guide to restaurants or places of entertainment. Such information can be obtained by writing to the chambers of commerce in the various cities.

What this book does try to do is to provide a selection of superb and relatively little-known public areas which can be visited easily and enjoyed immensely. There are references also to many other publicly owned areas which may have equal attraction, particularly in Chapter 7, so that the reader can still have the fun of some exploration and discovery on his own. Suggestions on how to improve this book in future editions, including comments on accommodations or other practical advice, would be most gratefully received and should be sent to the author, c/o J. B. Lippincott Company, 521 Fifth Avenue, New York, N.Y. 10017

The guide is divided into three parts. The first part is a general introduction to the Southwest, with material on its natural history, its early inhabitants, the conflict between the pioneers and the Indians, the colorful tales of the wild West, and the Indians who live there and carry on their ancient traditions today. The second part describes ten areas that should be visited by anyone looking for the quiet enjoyment of a place of beauty and wonder. The third part is a practical how-to-do-it section for the neophyte outdoorsman, designed to encourage city dwellers to brave the adventure of camping out—an activity which is much more pleasant and easy than one might suppose. A final chapter offers suggestions for noncampers who prefer stopping at motels.

I would like to add very special thanks to Agnes Marquette and Reta Thompson for their skill, patience, and, above all, enthusiasm in typing the manuscript. I would also like to thank my family: my husband, who cracked the whip, and our two daughters, Tryntje and Gabriel, who gave up a lot of skiing and other family outings so this book might be written.

I hope that the result will provide a starting place for many exciting trips into this beautiful territory by people who will respond to its splendor and its magic and who will want to join in helping to protect and preserve this great American heritage.

C. T. E. S.

New York
Spring, 1973

PART ONE
This Is the Southwest

1
The Pioneer Tradition

The Southwest is still an American frontier, where the air is clean, the scenery is wild and beautiful, and man has not yet been able to tame or destroy the freedom of the open spaces. The Southwest frontier still beckons Americans to visit and taste its excitement and wonder, at least for a brief moment. With four-lane interstate highways and frequent supermarkets, there are no longer the privations of thirst and starvation that faced the ill-fated Donner-Reed Party, but there is still enough of an air of adventure and of the unknown to bring out a twinge of the pioneer spirit in anyone.

In 1846, George and Jacob Donner and James Frazier Reed organized a wagon train of eighty-seven emigrants for a trek across the continent to California. They were families mostly from Illinois and Iowa. The Donner brothers were both over sixty years of age; Reed was forty-six. Six of the children were only one year old. When they reached the mountains, the wagon drivers spent two weeks trying to move through a steep canyon, only to find the route impassable. They changed course and moved through another canyon which led them into the bleak Salt Lake Valley. In early September the wagon train started across the parched Salt Lake Desert. After two and a half days without water, Reed rode ahead in search of a water supply which he located 30 miles beyond, at Pilot Peak. When he came back for the rest of the party he found that they still had 20 miles to go and that already the oxen were falling one by one. Reed's own wagon mired down and he was forced to abandon it. He and his wife carried their small children as they began to walk the rest of the way on foot. Eventually they became exhausted and accepted the nearness of death on the desert.

Meanwhile the Donners had reached Pilot Peak and Jacob Donner started back for the Reed family, finding them in time to save their lives. Many wagons were abandoned during the trek across the desert, and many of the cattle died, but the people survived. When they reached the Sierra Nevadas, however, they faced even worse obstacles. It was now so late in the year that the mountain snows had begun to fall, and the party found itself snowbound a scant hundred miles from Sutter's Fort. Forty-three of the eighty-seven died of starvation and exposure. The remainder survived by cooking and eating their boots, their harnesses, and the dead. The Donner-Reed story still lives in the annals of Western emigration as one of the most tragic losses in the pioneer movement.

Undaunted by tales of such tragedies, Western pioneers pressed on in increasing numbers. A few months after the Donner-Reed experience, Brigham Young led the first of the Mormon pioneers into the Salt Lake Valley, where they establishd a settlement that would one day be a good-sized city. In the following years, pioneers moved into other parts of the vast Western and Southwestern wilderness, establishing settlements and becoming part of the tradition of the land. In terms of Mormons alone, 80,000 started across the plains and mountains before the railroads were built. Over 6,000 of them lost their lives along the way. Today many more than a million descendants of these early pioneers live in the communities laid out by the original builders of the West.

At a meeting of the American Historical Association at the Chicago World's Fair in 1893, a young history professor from the University of Wisconsin read a paper on the significance of the frontier in American history which, since then, has had a dramatic impact on the whole historical evaluation of the settlement of the West. Frederick Jackson Turner altered the course of American historical scholarship with his thesis that American development is primarily explained by the advance of westward settlement. Turner asserted that the frontier fostered democracy and freed Americans from the influences and restrictions of the Old World. The challenge of the frontier required men to rid themselves of old institutions and customs, he said, as they adapted to the new environments they had to meet—social, political, and economic. The static social organization of Europe was thereby abandoned, and man had to learn to adopt new standards and rules to meet the conditions of an unorganized society.

Industry, initiative, individual enterprise, and ingenuity became primary values on the frontier. Optimism and resourcefulness were essential for men to survive. As each wave of pioneers pushed the frontier forward, American society underwent additional changes and refinement. Variations in the geographical make-up of the country contributed to the rise of sectionalism, reasoned Turner. But above all, the West provided a safety valve for American democracy. The dominant merchants and professional classes in the East were forced to make concessions to the blue-collar classes equal to the appeal of the freedom and economic opportunity that always awaited them in the open lands to the west. The frontier, in short, explains America.

Whether Turner was right or wrong, there is no question but that the frontier of the West has always brought a tingle of excitement to Americans, young and old. Although it has been "settled" for many decades, its spirit still lives in the land. Nature is still the dominant force in the frontier philosophy, and humans are only temporary inhabitants for the most fleeting seconds in time.

This book is about that part of the Southwest known as the Colorado Plateau—a great raised area covering portions of Utah, Colorado, New Mexico, and Arizona, with its center where those four states join together and extending about half a state in each direction. The Colorado Plateau region has the advantage of presenting some of the most varied scenery in the world while at the same time, because of its generally higher elevation, avoiding some of the extreme temperatures of the Southwestern desert lands. This does not mean that there are not desert temperatures on the plateau, but the variety and interest of the area more than make up for occasional discomforts.

According to one tall tale about the Southwestern climate, a cowboy decided to go for a swim one hot day, took off his clothes, walked to the edge of a cliff overlooking a stream, and dove in. As he jumped, a drought dried up the stream, but, just in time, a sudden flash flood roared down the dry creek bed, and the cowboy landed safely in the water. By the time he came up for air, however, a northeaster had suddenly blown up and frozen the surface of the water into solid ice. The cowboy would surely have drowned if the sun had not quickly reappeared and evaporated the stream. The only mishap from the experience was that the cowboy got a bad sunburn before he was able to get his clothes back on again.

Although the meteorological changes in actuality may not be quite so sudden, there are certainly wide variations in the weather of the Southwest. In the mountains, one may contend with hailstorms which often pelt down hailstones the size of old-fashioned mothballs. Snow remains on many of the mountain peaks while the temperature in the desert areas rises to 110 degrees and more. Regular rainstorms range through the area, and because of the great sweep of visibility it is common to see a dark cloud with gray sheets of rain streaming below it in some far corner of the sky every afternoon. It can pour torrents on one side of the road and be absolutely dry on the other side. Heavy rains at higher altitudes often contribute to the flash floods which have been known to hit unwary campers who mistakenly set up camp in dry stream beds. All things considered, however, the variety of the climate in the Southwest makes it quite agreeable for the visitor, and one should not be frightened off from a summer vacation trip because of a belief that the temperatures will be intolerable. They are quite tolerable and, indeed, often delightful.

The special climate of the Southwest has contributed to one of its unique characteristics: the adobe house. This type of construction, utilizing oversized bricks of sun-baked clay mixed with straw, was quickly taken over from the Indians by the pioneer settlers. Log cabins were seldom built in the Southwest. Timber was hard to come by and was not a building material suited to the climate. Thick adobe walls provide coolness in the summer and hold in warmth during the winter.

What will the modern-day pioneer find in the Southwest? Wonders beyond imagining: scenery and open space that cannot be believed till seen; Indians, still living by traditions of many centuries; rocks and minerals of striking beauty, some of which can be freely collected in certain areas; birds and animals of remarkable interest and beauty; trees and, above all, wild flowers growing in surprising profusion; a history of the land which stretches back beyond comprehension; a history of man, dramatically visible in archaeological ruins and artifacts; contemporary native arts and crafts with a very special excellence of their own; walks and trails to enjoy on foot or horseback; subject matter beyond wildest dreams for the artist or photographer; and people of a special breed, who are thoughtful and courteous and yet robust and colorful.

The scenery of the Southwest ranges from great stretches of flat desert sands to rugged mountain peaks, with canyons and rock formations of every conceivable shape, size, and color. Certain areas are overwhelming in size and scope, like the Grand Canyon. Others are scaled down as if intended by nature to be enjoyed by man, such as Canyon de Chelly. Mesas, buttes, spires, and cliffs all become familiar sights.

Thousands of Indians make their homes on the reservations of the Southwest. The term "Indian," of course, was the general name given by the first European explorers of the American continent to the many different peoples whom they found here, mistakenly believing, at first, that they had reached the East Indies. The name stuck, but the American Indians are actually many separate nations and tribes as diverse as the Irish and the French, the Swedish and the Spanish, the Germans and the Chi-

Canyon de Chelly

nese. Principal in numbers in the Southwest is the Navajo tribe, which also has made a substantial cultural contribution, building on its own traditions as well as many practices borrowed from other Indians in the past. Also living there are the Hopis, who, perhaps more than any of the others, continue to keep pure their ancient ways. Pueblo Indians occupy a string of communities along the Rio Grande River in northern New Mexico. The Zuñis and the Utes have reservations as well, as also do smaller groups of Apaches, Paiutes, and others. There are no fences around the reservations. Visitors are free to come and go. But there are invisible fences in the communities inhabited by the Indians and in their private lives. Most of them continue to resist the white man's invasion, even in their economic lives. A great deal is made of the economic progress of modern Indians, and that development is to be applauded in the light of their near-abject poverty only a few years ago. But the real message of Indian life in the Southwest today is the maintenance of a degree of integrity and continuity in the old traditions and arts. These are still there for the visitor to discover, and, although he may view many aspects of Indian life only from a distance, at least he can feel that he has a new awareness of its existence and reality.

The Southwest is a treasure trove of rocks and minerals. Petrified wood is found in many parts of the area. Striking displays may be seen at the Petrified Forest National Park, but specimens, often for sale, also appear more casually in gas stations, curio shops, and many other unexpected quarters. Found widely in the Southwest are iron pyrites, calcite, gypsum, and some turquoise. Quartz occurs in many forms: opal, chalcedony, agate, jasper, rose quartz, crystal quartz, and amethyst. The ores of the Southwest, in addition to gold and silver, include zinc, lead, copper, uranium, and fluorite. Some of the forms of copper ore are particularly beautiful as specimens. Sedimentary rocks are primarily sandstone and limestone. And metamorphic rocks include gneiss and schist. Igneous rocks are particularly frequent in the Southwest, including granite, diabase, felsite, obsidian, pumice, and basalt. There are many places in the Southwest where one is permitted to collect specimens, particularly in Utah. But for those who will not brave the rigors of climbing the slopes looking for choice items to take back home, numerous rock shops offer splendid specimens at very reasonable prices. In southwestern Utah, there are shops which have dooryards piled high with mineral specimens that are sold by the pound. In central Arizona, one may purchase handsome pieces of petrified wood for very nominal sums.

There is a Shoshoni Indian legend about the time the whole earth was covered with water and everything perished except for two birds who held onto the sky with their beaks. One bird was tiny, and the other was large and gray. As the waters rose, the large bird, being a coward, began to cry and almost lost his hold. The little bird held on tightly and whispered words of encouragement. When the waters receded, both birds were saved. Today, according to the legend, the children of the small bird fill the land with song, and the children of the large gray bird which showed fear can only make cries.

The Southwest is home to a great variety of the birds that sing and the birds that make cries. The most unusual form of animal life to be seen there are the lizards, which come in many shapes and colorations. All are harmless except the Gila monster, which one is not likely to run across in the ordinary course of things. Lizards are fascinating to watch, because of their natural camouflage and sudden movements. There are also a number of snakes, most of which are harmless (with the exception of rattlesnakes and coral snakes). A large dose of common sense is the principal protection against unwanted experiences with snakes. One simply does not step too close to dark shaded places or clumps of plant life where a snake might lurk undetected. Although there are many wild mammals in the Southwest, the casual visitor is most likely to see mule deer. These graceful creatures are quite numerous, and an early morning drive or hike in many of the park areas described in this book is likely to provide a close-up view of one or more of this species. The deer may also be seen on occasion in the early evening when they move around looking for food. Among the smaller animals, one may see chipmunks and ground squirrels, as well as occasional prairie dogs and jack rabbits.

Trees in the Southwest range from the conifers in the mountains to the cottonwoods of the canyons. The most delightful plant-life discovery in the Southwest is the wide range of wild flowers which can be found at all levels, from desert to mountains.

The Southwest gives one a humbling sense of perspective on the relative importance of human life in the scale of time. One suddenly finds oneself in the presence of rock formations which came into being hundreds of millions of years ago. Places which can be easily visited reach back over spans of time that stagger the imagination. Bear in mind that the earth's crust was formed two to three billion years ago, as the surface of the earth gradually cooled and the continents and the oceans developed. Approximately one billion years ago the earth was subjected to great eruptions and huge lava flows. Mountains were uplifted and then worn away. (Some of the rocks formed during this geologic period of time provide part of the now visible base of the Grand Canyon and the Black Canyon of the Gunnison.) Then the climate grew colder. Glaciers formed to the north. Seas and swamps spread over much of what is now the Southwest with alternate flooding and erosion. Thick sediments were laid down by the seas. (During this period the sandstone which can be seen in Canyon de Chelly was formed.) The final spread of the seas took place between 100 and 200 million years ago (forming some of the rocks which are now exposed at Mesa Verde, Arches, Capitol Reef, and Zion national parks). Then came the great period of mountain building, during the span from 10 to 70 million years ago, as the Rocky Mountains were pushed up and a number of volcanoes became active in the area. (This was the period in which the Petrified Forest and Bryce Canyon came into existence, and also the Great Sand Dunes.)

Against the backdrop of this long period of geologic evolution, man's presence in the area has been but a flicker of time. The earliest inhabitants of the Southwest are believed to have been nomadic hunters who roamed the region between ten thousand and twenty-five thousand years ago. In relatively modern times, the immediate forebears of the Southwestern Indians migrated to the area from Asia. Over the course of two thousand years these people have evolved into the present-day Pueblo Indians, with contributions along the way resulting from invasions by other tribes. The Pueblo Indian culture reached its high point in the Southwest while Europe was still in the Dark Ages. It might well have gone on to greater heights, but the arrival of the Spanish in 1540 turned its development to other directions with the introduction of new ideas and materials and livestock, notably horses and cattle.

There are a number of satisfying activities in which the modern-day visitor to the Southwest can participate. One of these, of course, is shopping for representative arts and crafts. The traditional Indian craftwork includes baskets, pottery, and kachina dolls, the wonderfully fashioned depictions of the Hopi messengers of the gods. If you have an interest in these things, many superb examples are still being made and can be purchased for moderate prices. Some of the larger kachina dolls, which usually sell for prices ranging from $30 to $75, make handsome decorative pieces, particularly in a modern setting. They are not mere curiosities but a true form of native folk art. More recent handicraft developments have been the Navajo rugs, which are

Hopi Kachina: Spirit of Sun God

particularly well suited for wall hangings, and the silver jewelry of the Navajos, Hopis, and Zuñis. Each of these is different from the others in its special characteristics, and each has its admirers. If you shop with caution and common sense, it is possible to purchase beautifully made examples of this work. There are many good shops handling these items, and shopping can be a major part of one's visit.

Another area of personal involvement in a visit to the Southwest is photography. Depending on one's interest, the range of subject matter is immense. Wild flowers, rugged country, sunsets, sweeping views, close-ups of nature—all are there. The sunlight is brilliant and the air is clear, so that photographic conditions are usually excellent. Often the moving clouds help to add the dimension of light and shadow patterns, particularly in the canyons, which provide changing moods from minute to minute. The problem is not how to find enough subject matter to photograph; the problem is how to bring enough film.

Another activity in which almost every visitor can participate with pleasure is walking or riding on horseback along the many trails which have been laid out in the parks and monuments of the Southwest. These trails vary from the easy to the strenuous. There is something for everyone. Whatever your level of activity, however, the enjoyment which comes from going it on your own in a strange land is immense. Be sure to allow enough time in your planning to take some of these walks or rides. You cannot savor the true pleasures of the Southwest just from the seat of an automobile.

If you come from a city where life is impersonal and sometimes cold and harsh, you will be struck by one other aspect of the Southwest—the humanity and good will of the people. Whether it is a gas station attendant, a checker in the supermarket, or someone you stop to ask directions, the chances are that you will be pleased by the enthusiasm and cheerfulness of your brief encounter. Whether it is the air or the scenery or the lack of overcrowding, something special happens to people when they are in the Southwest that puts them on their best behavior. The only exceptions to the general friendliness are the Indians, who still have a well-founded skepticism about the intentions of white people coming into their country. They are not openly antagonistic, but neither do they go out of their way to be friendly. Some words of advice for visitors to Indian country are included in Chapter 6.

As you visit the various parks and monuments you will be particularly impressed by the National Park Service personnel you encounter. Most Park Service employees are not only courteous and thoughtful but downright bounding in their enthusiasm and wholesomeness. You cannot get away from the feeling that one of the finest things we have accomplished in the history of this Republic is the establishment of national parks and the National Park Service, with its dedicated, earnest personnel who are concerned first and foremost with the protection of the land placed in their care and secondly with your pleasure and enjoyment of its beauties. That is really what the Southwest is all about.

2
Natural History

"It's a hell of a place to lose a cow," commented Ebenezer Bryce, as his arm made a sweeping gesture toward the twisted rock shapes that form multihued amphitheaters on the fringe of the Colorado Plateau in southwestern Utah. The place would one day be a national park named in his honor, but to farmer Bryce the practical problems of pasturing his cattle in the country he once hoped to develop for agricultural purposes overcame any preoccupation with its wild natural beauty.

GEOLOGICAL DEVELOPMENT

Although practical considerations still play a part in the lives of those who live there, the beauty that nature has wrought is plainly the dominant feature of the land. To appreciate that beauty fully requires some basic knowledge of the geological evolution of the Southwest. The facts are not complicated, but they need mastering if one is to understand the sweep of time embraced by rock formations, canyons, mesas, and mountains which dominate the landscape.

There are five basic periods of geologic time which are helpful to know:

I. The Archeozoic era, also known as Early Precambrian:

26

from two to three billion years ago, when the earth's crust was gradually being formed and the continents and oceans were beginning to take shape.

II.   The Proterozoic era, also known as Later Precambrian: running between five hundred million and one billion years ago, a period of great eruptions, lava flows, and uplifting and wearing away of mountains.

III.   The Paleozoic era: 180 to 250 million years ago, a period of flooding and sedimentation, alternating with erosion and glaciation.

IV.   The Mesozoic era: 60 to 180 million years ago, the dinosaur age, with swamps and flooding by shallow seas.

V.   The Cenozoic era: from the present time back to sixty million years ago, a period of volcanic activity, erosion, sedimentation, and glaciers.

The Southwest provides opportunities to see physical evidence of each of these great epochs of time. At first it is hard to grasp the fact that you are in the presence of material that came into being hundreds of millions of years ago. Then a sense of profound humility and insignificance comes over you, as you realize that the whole period of "civilization" is but a momentary splash in the stream of time. These are some of the things that were going on during the great periods of the earth's development. As you think about these events, you should bear in mind

Bryce Canyon National Park

that remnants of all these periods of time are still visible to the naked eye in the Grand Canyon.

The secret of the Grand Canyon and much of the other canyon territory of the Southwest is a muddy stream, the Colorado River. The Colorado is the second longest river in the United States, and as a cutting tool it is unequaled. It flows rapidly, at speeds up to twenty miles an hour, carrying sand and silt. Half a million tons of abrasive material move past any fixed point in the Grand Canyon in an average day. As the Colorado Plateau was gradually lifted, the river ground away in its course, cutting through the layers of rock as it relentlessly moved on to the sea. The plateau has now been lifted up almost a mile in height, while the river has held its relative position by cutting its path through the rock layers. Today, as the Colorado River winds through the Grand Canyon, the rocks along the banks, known as Vishnu schist, are remnants of a period almost two billion years ago. Following up the canyon walls from the river, rock layers represent each successive period of time right to the present. Many of the other canyons in the Southwest also cover wide spans of time in one or more of the great geologic eras. Here, in a little more detail, are some of the events that these ancient watchmen have witnessed.

In the *Archeozoic era*, two to three billion years ago, the beginning of time for the earth's surface, there are no indications that life existed, but there are some evidences of rain, wind, clouds, bodies of water, and movement of the earth's surface. During this period volcanic lavas and sediments piled horizontal layers of rock several thousands of feet thick. These rock layers were folded with the cooling of the surface, the folds forming mountain ranges into which molten material was injected from below. In time, the high mountains were eroded to form a plain close to sea level, with only the roots of the mountains remaining. Tremendous heat and pressure metamorphosed both sedimentary and volcanic rock into a new form of rock called schist. Intruding into this dark-colored material are veins of lighter-colored granite or pegmatite caused by molten material filling up cracks in the bed.

In the *Proterozoic era*, 500 million to one billion years ago, is reflected the first direct evidence of life on the planet. During this epoch, a sea encroached on the desert plain from the west and laid down a series of sedimentary deposits: red shale several hundred feet thick, sandstone of varying colors over a thousand feet thick, and then a layer of volcanic igneous rock. In all, some twelve thousand feet of rock were laid down during this period. In many places, that rock is now completely worn away. A number of limestone reefs from this period still exist, formed with the help of early algae. There is other evidence of simple plant life in the rocks of this period, but no animal fossils have been clearly identified. Some of the rocks of this era can be seen in the Black Canyon of the Gunnison, as well as in the Grand Canyon.

In the *Paleozoic era*, from 180 to 500 million years ago, there were repeated cycles of sedimentation and erosion. During this era, mosses and ferns became abundant, and plants and fish life increased. Sandstone, shale, and limestone are the rocks of this period. In the layers may be found numerous fossils of trilobites, primitive arthropods which flourished for about 200 million years, during much of which time they were the dominant animals of the sea. Fossils of the first animals with backbones are found in formations laid down during this era, along with scales of armored fish and other sea creatures. In a later period during this era, fossilized tracks of early reptiles in the mud can also be found, as well as trails of insects and worms. Shelled creatures also were in evidence. Sandstone laid down in this period now forms the walls of Canyon de Chelly, as well as a number of other areas in the Southwest.

In the *Mesozoic era*, 60 to 180 million years ago, the first important period in the development of animals and plants took place. During this time, several thousand feet of sediments were laid down in the last great spreading of the inland seas. The era also included a long period of erosion, during which much of the Grand Canyon was cut away. This was the Age of Reptiles, when land plants first developed, the first birds appeared, and dinosaurs roamed the land. The remains of dinosaurs found in the Southwest indicate that the creatures who roamed the land during this era were 100 feet in length, with a weight of 35 or 40 tons. Tracks left behind in the sandstone record the fact that at least eight varieties of dinosaurs lived in the Southwest for some 60 million years. One set of tracks indicates an animal which took 15-foot strides. Toward the end of this era, the great sea which extended over the land withdrew, and lateral pressure from the west folded the earth's crust into a series of mountains. In time, these early ancestral Rockies were largely eroded by wind and rain. Rock formations from the Mesozoic era can still be seen in Zion, Capitol Reef, Arches, and Mesa Verde national parks, and in the Painted Desert.

In the *Cenozoic era,* from the present time back to 60 million years ago, there has been an extended period of erosion, during which much of the rock laid down in the preceding eras has been worn away and the Grand Canyon itself has been cut deep into its ancient base. In the past million years of the present era, a substantial amount of volcanic activity has reappeared. Specific examples of the changes in the earth's crust that have taken place in the Cenozoic era include the Great Sand Dunes, the Petrified Forest, and Bryce Canyon. This, of course, is also the Age of Mammals and of the gradual evolution of life on the planet as we know it today.

A familiar geologist's device for stating these periods of time in understandable terms is to portray the two billion years of the earth's geologic history as a single twenty-four-hour day. Starting at midnight, the day runs through until the following noon before the first era of creation is completed and the earth moves into the Proterozoic era, when primitive water plants in the form of algae first appear. By evening, the Paleozoic era has arrived, when the oceans are filled with a variety of marine organisms, but still no life has appeared on land. As night sets in, amphibians, reptiles, and dinosaurs come and go among the ferns, and birds and mammals appear. Ten seconds before 11:53 P.M., the erosion of the Grand Canyon begins. Ancient man appears on the African continent at 11:59 and 17 seconds.

Despite the presence of rock formations going back to the

beginning of the earth's history, the Colorado Plateau, which comprises the principal part of the Southwest about which this book is written, is still a relatively busy area in terms of its geological activity, since water has only recently begun to erode it. In the coming centuries the canyons will widen and the material washed from the canyon walls will be carried away by the Colorado River and its tributaries. Geologists predict that in the next several million years these streams will carve the plateau into a series of ridges and buttes, until the entire landscape resembles Monument Valley on the border of Arizona and Utah, where remnants of an earlier plateau can be seen in scattered outcroppings. Until the next uplifting of the land, the process of erosion will continue to work away on the Colorado Plateau and will eventually level it again to a single plain close to sea level, repeating the same cycle which has occurred so many times before.

Not everyone accepts the geologists' technical explanation for the land forms and rocks in the Southwest. The Indians, particularly, have quite a different view of how these things came about. Take, for example, Shiprock, a volcanic plug located in northwestern New Mexico, rising abruptly some 1,400 feet above the surrounding plain and resembling a sailing ship under way. The geologists explain that Shiprock is what remains of an old vol-

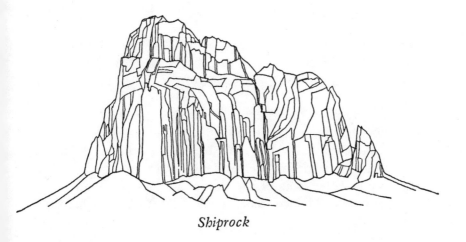

Shiprock

cano which eroded away, leaving bare the hard core of rock formed from the molten lava which had plugged its throat at the end of its active period. The Navajo Indians, on the other hand, call this igneous rock formation "the winged rock" and regard it as a sacred mountain. According to Navajo legend, the tribe was once under siege by the Utes. The Navajos were in desperate straits when the medicine men of the tribe decided to seek divine help and organized a ceremony which ran on for two full days, with all of the tribal members participating. On the evening of the second day, as the Navajos prayed and chanted, the ground beneath them suddenly rose up into the air, with rocky crags protruding as wings on either side, and sailed off across the plains, leaving the confused enemy behind. The rocky outcrop sailed on and on through the night until sundown of the following day, when it came to rest in the middle of the open plain.

PLANT LIFE

One of the great surprises the first-time visitor encounters in the Southwest is the abundance of wild flowers. Many people think of wild flowers in terms of the Eastern Seaboard of the United States, but in fact they grow in far greater profusion and color in the Southwest, where they are found virtually everywhere through the summer months. There is also a variety of other remarkable plant life, including numerous kinds of that curious phenomenon the cactus, as well as handsome localized trees such as the cottonwood, the pungent-smelling juniper, the revered piñon, and the great stands of evergreens in the mountain forests.

The early pioneers made much practical use of the supply of plant life they found. Jams and jellies were made from the fruit of the chokeberry as well as other berries and wild currants. The leaves of the dandelion were eaten, as were the bulbs of the sego lily and the roots of the thistle. Various plants and roots were ground and boiled to make colored dyes. Weeds and dried bushes were used for brooms. Some cattails and other plants served as stuffing for mattresses and cushions. Remedies for certain ailments were concocted from prickly pears and dandelion roots. Some of the more adventurous pioneers compounded a form of chewing gum from the juice of the milkweed. And the sap in the inner bark of cottonwood trees was scraped together in a pulpy mass called "cottonwood ice cream."

In order to enjoy the plant life of the Southwest more fully, one should obtain a good pocket handbook or two. Among the more useful paperbacks which are quite widely available are: *Trees of North America,* a Golden Field Guide ($2.95); *A Pocket Guide to Trees,* by Rutherford Platt (75¢); and *The Southwest,* a Golden Regional Guide ($1.95). The listings that follow are designed to give a general indication of those plants which are most frequently found, so that easy reference to a handbook can be made.

Wild flowers are abundant throughout the Southwest, whether on the desert, on the mesas, or in the mountains. They are mostly yellow, blue, white, and pink. These are some of the most common varieties:

DESERT FLOWERS	MESA FLOWERS	MOUNTAIN FLOWERS
Arizona lupine	Evening primrose	Colorado columbine
Gold poppy	Locoweed	Harebell
Desert marigold	Gaillardia	Western yarrow
Sacred datura	Calabazilla	Leafy-bract aster
Prickly poppy	Wild zinnia	Skyrocket gilia
Wild potato	Blazing star	Richardson geranium
Sand verbena	Snakeweed	Shooting star
Brittlebush	Golden crownbeard	Spreading fleabane
Desert senna	Palmer penstemon	Columbia monkshood
Filaree	Rocky Mountain bee plant	Gentian
Purple mat		
Paper flower		

Of all the botanical curiosities in the Southwest, the cactus is probably the most unusual. Contrary to popular belief, the cactus is not limited to arid desert regions but can be found in many parts of North, Central, and South America, in jungles, near seashores, on plains, and even in mountains. The principal characteristic of the cactus which explains its ability to survive the hardest climate is the layer of wax which coats the outer bark and serves to stem evaporation, making it possible for some species of cactus to live as long as two years without a drop of rainfall. The root system of the cactus draws in such water as can be found and transforms it into a mucilaginous substance, much thicker than the sap found in leafy plants, which is then drawn up into the storage cells of the plant, where it is held until needed during periods of drought. Cacti adjust themselves to their environment to such an extent that the skin tissues on the southerly sides of the plants are toughened to withstand the hot sun while the skin to the north is much more sensitive. Amateur transplanting often causes the death of a cactus plant which is not placed in exactly the same relative position as that in which it was originally found. When the plant is turned around, the northerly side may receive a bad sunburn, resulting in the rotting and death of the cactus. Unlikely as it seems, the cactus produces edible fruit, some of which make delicious candies and jellies, particularly the juicy red fruit of the prickly pear. The sweet fruit of the giant saguaro cactus serves as a staple in the Indian diet. Other cacti produce fruits which provide sustenance to birds and animals. A detailed guide, *Cacti of the Southwest* by W. Hubert Earle, is available in many of the national parks and may also be purchased from the Desert Botanical Gardens, P.O. Box 5415, Phoenix, Arizona 85010.

Shrubs are also an important part of the plant life of the Southwest and are found on each level of the terrain. Many of them bear flowers and berries and provide special benefits for people and animals. This is a listing of the most common shrubs, for ease in referring to an appropriate handbook for detailed identification data:

DESERT SHRUBS	MESA SHRUBS	MOUNTAIN SHRUBS
Creosote bush	Utah serviceberry	Buckbrush
Saltbush	Big sagebrush	Western thimbleberry
Mormon tea	Rabbit brush	Water birch
Wolfberry	Apache plume	Arizona mountain ash
Mescal		Wild raspberry
Jojoba		Chokecherry
Fairy duster		Alder-leaved mountain mahogany
Smoke tree		Poison ivy
Yucca		Low juniper
Century plant		

Except in the mountain forests, splendid with tall evergreens, one is not struck by the trees of the Southwest as much as by the wild flowers and shrubs. There are some exceptions, however. One is the cottonwood tree, which can grow to a handsome old age, with gnarled trunk and deep green foliage. Another is the juniper, which, when loaded with berries, has not only beauty but the haunting smell of a martini cocktail about it. Then, perhaps most intriguing of all, is the piñon. This tree, rejected by commercial loggers because of its twisted, gnarled branches, is one of the most important forms of plant life for the Indians of the Southwest. From the days of the cliff dwellers, the root of the piñon tree has been a major source of fuel, and even today, in the summertime, one can see Indian families collecting the wood from the countryside to store it up for the coming winter. A particular delicacy produced by the tree is the piñon nut, the seed which grows in the pine cone. An important source of food for wildlife, piñon nuts are also greatly relished by the Indians, who gather them as a harvest crop in September and October. They can be purchased in many of the trading posts, and a bag of them is well worth the small investment. Here is a listing of some of the common trees that can be found in the Southwest:

DESERT TREES	MESA TREES	MOUNTAIN TREES
Tesota	Utah juniper	White fir
Yellow paloverde	Rocky Mountain	Spruce
Catclaw acacia	juniper	Douglas fir
Mesquite	One-seed juniper	Ponderosa pine
Desert willow	Alligator juniper	Limber pine
Tamarisk	Piñon	Alpine fir
Arizona cypress	Inland box elder	Bristlecone pine
Arizona sycamore	New Mexican locust	Alder
	Narrow-leaved	Quaking aspen
	cottonwood	Peachleaf willow
	Gambel oak	Rocky Mountain
		maple

ANIMAL LIFE

For those who associate summertime with mosquitoes, the Southwest is a happy discovery. There are virtually no mosquitoes to be found. There are places where flies can be quite annoying, but by and large, the insect pests associated with other parts of the country do not exist here. This does not mean that there are no insects. Indeed, there are many different kinds of insects in the Southwest, some of them fascinating and a few of them menacing. Those most likely to be encountered by the visitor are the cicada, whose shrill, vibrating song one may hear on hot summer days; the sphinx moth and the yucca moth, which are likely to appear in the evening; the stinging fire ant and other ants which one may suddenly come upon in energetic colonies; and the kissing bug, an unusual black creature whose bite is extremely unpleasant. There are also several varieties of bees, including the cumbersome bumblebee and the honeybee. Honeybees are kept throughout the Southwest and down into Mexico, and one will often notice their boxlike hives dotting the countryside along the road. There are some other odd creatures in the insect family, among which are the walking stick, marvelously camouflaged as a twig, and the box-elder bug (found, as you might guess, near the tree of the same name) which will stand on its head if threatened. There are numerous beetles, and there are wasps, two of which are worthy of mention here. One is the tarantula hawk, whose name derives from its habit of preying on those huge spiders to feed its young. The other is the velvet ant, a wasp despite its name. If one is lucky, one may see one of these flightless wasps making its way across the desert floor like a tiny, bright-colored, walking pincushion. It is not advisable to pick it up, however, since its sting is not so appealing as its appearance. On the whole, one can regard insects in the Southwest with interest rather than with apprehension, although common sense should be the rule in dealing with them.

The Southwest is a Garden of Eden for bird watchers. Birds are numerous and colorful at all levels of the land, but probably nowhere more satisfying than in the mountain forests. A good pocket handbook such as *Birds of North America*, a Golden Field Guide ($2.95), is invaluable for real enjoyment of bird watching, and a pair of binoculars is also desirable. Here are some of the more common species one is likely to see:

DESERT BIRDS	MESA BIRDS	MOUNTAIN BIRDS
Phainopepla	Rock wren	Mountain chickadee
Cactus wren	Black-billed magpie	Hairy woodpecker
Sparrow hawk	Mourning dove	Mountain bluebird
Loggerhead shrike	Western meadowlark	Calliope hummingbird
Road runner	Golden eagle	Blue grouse
Gila woodpecker	Say's phoebe	Dipper
Ash-throated flycatcher	Scrub jay	Brown-capped rosy finch
Common nighthawk	Piñon jay	White-breasted nuthatch
Crissal thrasher	Brown towhee	Clark's nutcracker
Gambel's quail	Burrowing owl	Steller's jay
	Red-tailed hawk	

The Southwest plays host to many of that family of primitive creatures the reptiles. Reptiles fall into four broad groups: snakes, lizards, tortoises, and alligators and crocodiles. Of these groups, the two primarily found in the Southwest are snakes and lizards, although there are some tortoises in the desert regions. Although many people shudder instinctively when they think of reptiles, the fact is that once a little effort is made to understand them they become some of the most fascinating of living things. It is important, simply, to use caution while approaching them.

The dry, tough skin of reptiles permits them to retain moisture, so that they can exist for long periods of time with little access to water. Some reptiles never need to drink at all, obtaining their moisture from their food supplies. Reptiles hibernate and apparently are quite gregarious in their habits of hibernation. One unusual scientific study of a hibernation den over a ten-year period produced this remarkable inventory of its winter occupants, making a total of 1,730 snakes over the decade-long span:

930 western rattlesnakes
632 striped whipsnakes
127 racers
 36 gopher snakes
  2 night snakes
  2 regal ringneck snakes
  1 long-nosed snake

Although snakes are the most dramatic of the reptiles, one is much more likely to encounter a few lizards during his visit to the Southwest than to run across any snakes. Lizards usually have four legs, and their toes and claws are adapted to the energetic climbing, digging, and running which characterize their movements. The most remarkable physical feature of the lizard is its tail, which is commonly arranged so that it will separate neatly from its owner's body when caught in the jaws of some predator, permitting the lizard itself to escape. The separated tail immediately begins to writhe frantically and distracts the enemy while the balance of the animal makes its escape. A new tail grows in a very short time.

As you walk the trails, stay alert for sudden flashes of movement out of the corner of your eye, and you will most likely see a lizard. If you are observant, you will see that even among lizards there is wide variation in size, shape, and color, from the squat and chunky short-horned lizard (often called horned toad) to the several kinds of whiptails which are the ultimate in streamlined design.

Although one should not become alarmed about remote possibilities, neither should one be foolish about the fact that there are some poisonous creatures in the desert. There are three poisonous rattlesnakes and a deadly coral snake that should be treated with respect. No one has yet recorded the bite of a coral snake, but there have been a number of bites by rattlers. Other poisonous inhabitants of the Southwest include the Gila monster, the only poisonous lizard, a large creature with bead-like scales and a thick tail which is unmistakable in its appearance; the tarantula, a big, hairy brown spider whose bite is more painful than serious; the desert centipede; the black widow spider; and the scorpion. In the national parks, help is usually close at hand, but if one is going off on a camping trip into isolated country it is wise to study the problem of poisonous creatures more seriously and take along a snake-bite kit. A few rules of common sense will minimize any risks: if you are camping on the ground, always be sure to shake out your bedding and clothing; when you are walking on the trails, be sure to wear stout hiking shoes with leather uppers (not sneakers); watch where you walk, and avoid stepping near dark shadowy places under bushes or rocks.

Most of the wild mammals in the Southwest are of the smaller variety. There are a few of the larger species still in existence, but most, like the buffalo that once roamed the plains in the thousands, are either extinct or carefully nurtured in small herds on special preserves; occasionally, a mangy individual will be found on display in a zoo. The largest mammal one is likely to see while traveling through the Southwest is the mule deer, which can often be found in the early morning or at dusk along many of the quieter roads. Other large to middle-sized mammals which still live in the Southwest but are only rarely seen by visitors are pronghorns, bighorn sheep, cougars, gray foxes, coyotes, and bobcats.

In contrast to the scarcity of the larger mammals, the small mammals are everywhere, and many are a source of great pleasure and enjoyment. Among the more curious of the small creatures are the fabled pack rats, which have the odd habit of carrying off articles from campsites and replacing each one with some other object, such as a stick, a rock, or a piece of cactus. Many stories are told about mysteries caused by pack rat escapades. There was the partnership of prospectors that was almost dissolved because each member became suspicious of the others, as objects began to disappear. There is also the sad tale of a surveying team which came to a rude end when a pack rat made off with its only ruler, and the near-tragedy of the miner who almost tripped over six sticks of his own dynamite which had been moved by one of these nocturnal prowlers.

Of all the small mammals, however, none is more intriguing than the prairie dog. Once populating the Southwest in large numbers, prairie dogs are now to be found only occasionally, usually in national parks. These animals, which are neither dogs (they are actually a form of squirrel) nor residents of the prairie (they usually inhabit the grassy plains), have an organized social existence in their communities that would make many big-city mayors jealous. Each prairie dog town is divided up into individual precincts, each precinct being made up of a number of mounds and connecting tunnels. The mounds are usually about 2 feet high and 4 or 5 feet across, with upward of twenty such mounds to the acre. The burrow entrance leads into a precipitous tunnel which descends as much as 12 feet into the ground, where it turns at a sharp angle, continues for some distance, and then gradually rises. There are a number of branch tunnels off the main one, some containing grass-filled nests, others providing flood hatches, where the occupant can go for safety in the event of heavy rain. (If flooding fills up the tunnel, an air pocket is created in the flood hatch area.) When a prairie dog wanders into another precinct, the local residents start giving territorial yips, leaping into the air and almost falling over backward in their zeal. Other residents take up the cry, and soon the trespasser has no doubt that he is unwelcome. A similar yip is given as a warning of approaching danger and is also taken up by other residents to give their companions an opportunity to take cover. Predators most feared by the prairie dogs are ferrets, badgers, and hawks. Nature placed the prairie dog's eyes almost at the top of his head, so that he is equipped to scan the skies when first sticking his head out of his burrow hole. In the spring, when the young arrive, a special form of population control is practiced by the prairie dogs. Some of the older residents move out into new territory to make room for the newcomers. With the spring rains, they dig into the soft earth and start new towns sufficient to keep both old and new population centers in proper balance.

Some of the smaller mammals one might encounter on a visit to the Southwest are the following:

DESERT MAMMALS	MESA MAMMALS	MOUNTAIN MAMMALS
Kangaroo rat	Pocket gopher	Mantled ground
Coati	Tufted-eared	squirrel
Kit fox	squirrel	Chipmunk
Ringtail	Prairie dog	Yellow-haired
	Black-tailed	porcupine
	jack rabbit	Marmot

Bird watchers and other nature lovers are regular visitors to the Southwest nowadays, but it was not always so. During the early mining days, when life was hardier and men lived by the gun and the bottle, a naturalist was an oddity. They tell a story in central Utah of a fellow named Little Billie King, who came into Eureka, Utah, around the turn of the century and brought with him a habit of heavy drinking. In the summertime, Billie frequently wandered off to a sunny hillside, where he would sleep off his latest drinking bout, thereby combining the therapy of perspiration with a good rest. One afternoon he awoke groggily from an alcoholic nap to see a man running across the hillside with what looked like a fish net, apparently trying to catch fish in mid-air. Billie decided to treat him with caution and understanding, and approached him friendly-like but firmly. The man explained that he was only searching for bugs to add to his collection of specimens, but his explanation increased Billie's suspicions. "Sure, I know," answered Billie, "I've had 'em myself. You'd better come to town with me." This time it was the stranger who decided he had better humor Billie, who was obviously insane, and agreed to go into town with him. There Billie learned the truth, that the man with the net was a distinguished entomologist named Tom Spalding, after whom twelve unusual specimens had been named, including a tiny blue butterfly, the first of its kind ever found.

3
The Early Inhabitants

On June 22, 1929, a partially burned and decayed piece of wood was found on the Hopi reservation which was destined to send waves of excitement throughout the scientific world. The non-descript treasure was found by Dr. Andrew E. Douglass, an astronomer-turned-archaeologist, who was in pursuit of speci-mens to support his theory that the age of archaeological ruins could be established from the rings on logs from trees. The science of tree-ring dating, formally known as dendrochronol-ogy, was developed by Dr. Douglass in the course of a study on the effects of sunspots on climatic conditions. Dr. Douglass had reasoned, since available meteorological records only went back a few years, that he could study climatic conditions by looking at the annual growth rings on pine trees. Each year a tree grows a new layer of wood, the size of which depends on the amount of food and moisture the tree received during the course of the year. When a tree is cut down, one can examine the rings of the tree in cross-section and see the variations in width of each ring, reflecting one year's growth and the amount of rainfall that occurred during that year. A dry year produces a narrow ring, a wet year, a wide one. The pine is particularly responsive to climatic change. And since pine trees live to a ripe old age, Dr. Douglass figured that by cutting down old trees he could learn what the climatic conditions were over the course of a good many years. Arizona was a particularly good setting for such research because of the variations in rainfall and the availability of pine trees.

Through his examinations of a number of living trees, Dr. Douglass learned that tree-ring patterns may be read quite precisely. Every tree that has lived through a particular year reflects the same picture of that year's climatic conditions, showing a ring of identical relative width with that of every other tree which lived through the same year in the same region. Having started with living trees, Dr. Douglass next began to examine trees which had been cut down a good many years before, and which had been growing during the period before the living trees had started their growth. By overlapping the ring patterns of these trees with those of the living trees he had first studied, he was able to extend his dating measurement to progressively older trees. Through examinations of log beams used in old construction, he was able to work his way back to a still earlier time. Over the course of extensive research, Dr. Douglass had established tree-ring patterns extending from the year 1929 all the way back to the year 1280. But then he was stymied. He could not get any farther back in time.

Meanwhile, Dr. Douglass had found in the timbers of old houses a number of small samples of older trees which he could relate to each other but could not fit into the over-all pattern. He had established a spread of 580 years through these various samples but had not been able to link them up to a fixed starting point. That enigma was what started him on the quest for the nondescript log he found on June 22.

Dr. Douglass and a group of research assistants decided to search for the missing link in the village of Oraibi on the Hopi Indian Reservation in northern Arizona. Oraibi, he knew, had been occupied continuously since long before the Spanish arrived in the sixteenth century. When he reached Oraibi, Dr. Douglass requested permission to take specimens from some of the pine beams of the oldest village houses. His request was not received with much enthusiasm until he produced a gift for the Head Man of yards and yards of purple chiffon velvet. This pleased the Head Man greatly and produced the desired results. Dr. Douglass was sensitive to the feelings of the Hopis and took great care in obtaining his specimens. One of the techniques his research team used was to bore into a beam and remove a small round plug about the size of a wooden pencil, along which the rings appeared clearly. In order to appease the Hopi Spirit of Decay, the archaeologist frequently placed bits of turquoise in the holes left by his borings.

One particular specimen found in Oraibi showed a pattern of tree rings extending from the year 1260 to the year 1344, when the tree was cut down to construct the dwelling. This meant, of course, that the dwelling had been inhabited for almost six hundred years, since it had been abandoned only a few years before the specimen was taken. Although many other beams were studied, there were no others whose inner rings predated 1300, and so Dr. Douglass and his associates moved on to the ruins of earlier villages which had been occupied by the Hopis before they had come to Oraibi. One of these was the ruin at Show Low, where discoveries of ancient pottery had indicated that the Hopis had been in residence many centuries before. It was at Show Low that Dr. Douglass discovered the partially burned beam, which received the identification number HH39. As the unprepossessing log was examined, the tree rings clearly established chronology going back to the year 1237. At the same time, the long span of rings, almost six hundred of them, provided a bridge to the previously undetermined sequence of 580 years that had been a puzzle to the scientists. HH39 became the key piece in the puzzle of American archaeology in the Southwest; it was now possible to establish the dates of construction and occupation of most of the ruins there. The life span of HH39 was of particular significance because it was in the latter part of the thirteenth century that the great drought occurred which contributed to the abandonment of the cliff dwellings at Mesa Verde. Dr. Douglass and his associates continued their researches and were ultimately able to set up a tree-ring measurement which extends all the way back to A.D. 11. But few of their discoveries have been as exciting or significant as that nondescript piece of wood found on the Hopi reservation in the summer of 1929.

MAN IN THE SOUTHWEST

High above the Colorado River, near Moab, Utah, is an ancient drawing chipped into the red sandstone walls which rise straight up from the river. It is a picture, 42 inches long and 14 inches high, of an animal with a short upturned trunk which scientists generally agree is a mastodon, a creature said to have been extinct for 30,000 years. There is reason to believe that this picture was carved by some early human inhabitant and may be

Ancient Petroglyphs on Rock near Canyonlands National Park

the earliest evidence of man's habitation in the Southwest. More certain evidence has been found in the Sandia Mountains of New Mexico, where excavations of a cave have yielded crude stone spear points and the bones of prehistoric horses, bison, camels, mastodons, and mammoths—presumably the remains of hearty meals eaten by ancient hunters who are believed to have lived there 25,000 years ago.

The most significant discovery relating to early man was made in 1926 at Folsom, New Mexico, where well-made stone spear points were first discovered along with the bones of an early bison, dating the human artifacts some 15,000 years ago. Prior to the 1926 find, all available evidence had indicated that man had first arrived in the Southwest only a few thousand years ago. The careful craftsmanship of the Folsom points indicates a high degree of skill among the people who lived and hunted there. These early workmen had learned the secret of flaking the hardened stone with fine precision. The correlation of these small bits of evidence, together with other archaeological discoveries in various other parts of the Southwest, has helped to fix the time when they were used.

Very little is known about the actual living conditions of these earliest residents. Presumably they did not build fixed dwelling places, or practice agriculture, or work in metal or pottery, since no remains of these have been found. Only two skeletons have been discovered which can be traced back any significant distance in time, and they differ very little from those of later Indians. Logic alone has been used to determine how man arrived in this hemisphere, the best guess being that waves of migration came from Asia via the Bering Strait, at the point where the North American and Asian continents are presently separated by only a few miles and connected by a string of islands. Groups may also have traveled through the Aleutians. Presumably these migrations from Asia continued repeatedly over long stretches of time, with the wanderers spreading down across the Southwest, in their search for a compatible climate and living conditions, and ending up in New Mexico.

The history of man in the Southwest is divided roughly into three broad periods. The first is the prehistoric, ranging from approximately 25,000 years ago to the start of the Christian era. During this time, man was an opportunist, living off the land, hunting game, and gathering wild fruits and berries. Most of our knowledge of this period comes from deduction and common sense, based largely on the finds of hunting points and similar artifacts which are all that remain of that era.

The second period runs from A.D. 1 to 1300, and the people

whose culture evolved through these centuries are commonly referred to as the Anasazi, after the Navajo word for "the ancient ones." The Anasazi culture embraced two significant developments in the evolution of human activity, the weaving and use of fine baskets and the organization of dwelling units into pueblos, or villages. These two achievements gave their names to periods within the main era: the Basketmaker and, later, the Pueblo. Unquestionably, the latter part of this era was the high point of cultural achievement by the indigenous residents of the Southwest. The quality of design in structures and utensils is remarkable, and the high level of good taste and creativity is truly outstanding.

The third broad historic period of man in the Southwest is the modern era, dating from A.D. 1300 and running on to the present. Although the white man intrudes into this period of history, what is relevant for the present chapter is the thread of development from the early residents to the Indians of today, who reflect all of the cultural advances spanning these three major historic units of time.

For a fuller understanding of the present-day Indian cultures in the Southwest, it will be useful to take a closer look at two of the most interesting earlier periods: the Basketmaker and the Pueblo.

Basketmaker Period (A.D. 1–750)

The event of greatest significance which marks the time of the Basketmakers was the development of agriculture. Instead of relying on the bounty of nature as it could be found in the countryside, man began to cultivate the land himself and thus to produce crops he could rely on. The two basic cultivated crops in the early part of the Basketmaker Period were corn and squash. Knowledge of agriculture apparently came from Central or South America, brought by Indians who had traveled south, seen its use, and then carried the knowledge farther and farther north. It is difficult today to realize the dramatic significance of man's developments in the Southwest during this period beginning approximately 2,000 years ago. The people were Indians much like those we know, and they apparently covered a wide area throughout Utah, Arizona, New Mexico, and Colorado. Their utensils reflect inventions which were every bit as important to them as the automobile and the dishwasher are to us today. Corn provided a major staple in the Basketmakers' diet. Its principal virtue was that it could be preserved throughout the winter for grinding, cooking, and eating as needed. Squash performed double duty, serving as food when it was fresh and providing gourd vessels for drink and foodstuffs throughout the year. These people did not limit themselves to squash, of course, but continued to use also the fruits and vegetables provided by nature, including berries, piñon nuts, acorns, seeds, roots, and bulbs. One archaeological find indicates that their diet included the fruit of the cactus—a researcher discovered a cactus seed in the decayed molar of a skull taken from a Basketmaker grave site.

The other principal cultural achievement of the people living in this period of time is reflected in their name. The evolution of the basket gave great flexibility to their mode of living. Baskets could be used for carrying water (when lined with pitch from the piñon tree), for storing food, and even for cooking. Researchers have reasoned that food was cooked in baskets filled with water which was heated by placing and replacing hot stones in it until it came to a boil.

The same skills that went into basketmaking also went into the making of other articles, including sandals, which increased the ability of early man to travel across the countryside by protecting his feet against bruises and cuts. With imaginative use of the various raw materials available to them, such as bone, wood, hair, and parts of certain plants, the Basketmakers achieved many remarkable advances. They made themselves fur robes by wrapping strings of yucca fibers with narrow strips of rabbit fur and then weaving them together. They fashioned snares and nets, as well as spears, to aid in their quest for food. In their nets they caught birds and small animals such as rabbits, prairie dogs, gophers, badgers, and field mice. They hunted larger animals, such as deer and mountain lions, with long darts propelled by a launching device known as an "atlatl," which functioned as a powerful extension of the arm, in much the same way as the stick used to carry and drive the ball in the game of lacrosse or the basket used for the same purpose in the Spanish game of jai alai. Larger game provided not only food but also skins and bone. Everything, in its way, performed an important functional service for the Basketmaker Indians.

These skillful artisans also gave attention to vanity and produced decorative pieces and things for personal adornment. Some of these things have been preserved, including comblike items which they made out of bone or feathers to decorate their hair. They fashioned beads for necklaces and ear pendants out of seeds, acorns, stones, bones, and even shells. Archaeologists are particularly intrigued by the discovery, among the traces left by the Basketmakers, of olivella and abalone shells normally found only along the Pacific coast, indicating a system of trade and barter during this period which covered long distances.

Archaeologists divide the Basketmaker Period into two distinct eras, one running from approximately A.D. 1 to 450, the other running from A.D. 450 to approximately 750. This later period is often referred to as the Modified Basketmaker Period. During this time organized villages comprised of houses and granaries evolved. The houses were shallow pits with roofs erected above them, something like basements with part below ground and part above.

During this later portion of the Basketmaker Period the manufacture of pottery began, apparently also learned from the Indians living to the south. The potter's wheel was never discovered in the Southwest. Instead, pottery was made by pressing the clay. One technique involved molding the clay inside baskets. Another involved the coiling of a long, thin roll of clay into the desired shape. Sometimes the vessel was left with the pattern made by the coil showing on the surface. Other times the clay was scraped smooth. Firing the pottery was achieved by a rather haphazard method. Pieces of unfired pottery were grouped together and then surrounded by firewood which was set alight. The number of unsuccessful firings must have been considerable, but out of it all has come a remarkable group of artifacts which provide leads to the way these people lived more than a thousand years ago.

Perhaps the most exciting collection of things dating back to the Basketmakers is displayed at the museum in Mesa Verde National Park. Here one can see excellent examples of various forms of weaving, pottery, hunting tools, and other articles made and used by the people of this time, as well as handsome baskets of all shapes and sizes. One display includes several beautiful and astonishingly well-preserved sashes braided out of dog hair. For more detail, see Chapter 15.

Pueblo Period (A.D. 750–1300)

According to an old Ute legend, the people who occupied the cliff dwellings in the Southwest were once animals who lived inside the earth and climbed to the upper world on a giant cornstalk. When they reached the surface, they took the form of human beings, but when they celebrated their deliverance in their underground kivas, or ceremonial chambers, they dressed themselves in the masks and skins of their ancestors. When the cliff dwellers began building their kivas above ground, they displeased the gods, who then withheld the rainfall and caused the great drought which led to the abandonment of the dwellings.

The real story of the development of the cliff dwellings is almost as intriguing as this imaginative version. The reason for their abandonment is still something of a mystery, although anthropologists surmise that a great drought, which is evidenced in the tree-ring patterns of the time, was the main stimulus for the departure of the cliff dwellers. After the time of the Basketmakers, the Indians of the Southwest continued to develop their culture with greater and greater refinement. Three principal achievements marked the new period, which has come to be known as the Pueblo Period. The most important of these was in the field of architecture. The Indians of the Pueblo Period transformed the earlier pit houses into dwellings built entirely above ground, while the ceremonial kivas were now built entirely below ground. In addition, these people constructed dance

courts, ovens, storage rooms, and summer shelters. Their architecture became increasingly dramatic as more and more people
clustered together into single communities, with subdivisons by
clans centered about the individual kivas, each of which served
just a few families. The Pueblo structures evolved into apartment
houses, at first located on the ground and later built into caves
high in the sides of cliffs for greater protection, presumably
against marauders.

The second striking achievement of the Pueblo Period was the
cultivation of cotton. The other basic cultivated plants still included corn and squash, as well as beans. Cotton, however, added
to the available materials for weaving cloth and provided new
comfort.

The third achievement of real significance in the Pueblo Period
was the refinement of pottery techniques and decoration. There
are few indigenous art forms more beautiful than the freehand
patterns reflected in the black-on-white pottery developed during
the latter part of the great Pueblo Period. Of equal beauty are
the corrugated-surfaced pots designed for storage and cooking.

During this same period of growth from 750 to approximately

Thirteenth-century Pueblo Storage Jar (Mesa Verde Museum)

1300, the Indians also refined their hunting instruments, developing the bow and arrow, and became much more elaborate in their bead making.

Then, toward the end of the Pueblo Period, over a number of years from 1276 to 1299, a calamity fell on this highly developed civilization. A disastrous drought, probably caused by a falling of the water table, afflicted the communities, and their whole farming economy collapsed. Slowly but surely the people abandoned their beautiful cliff homes and went in search of a more reliable source of water. One of the new communities they founded was in what is now Bandelier National Monument, through which ran, and still runs, a small but full-flowing river. The Indians carried with them what they could, but they also left many of their possessions behind. Although much was taken by later marauders, much has also remained for study and enjoyment by present-day visitors.

Modern Era (1300 to the present)

The modern era in Southwest Indian history is really little more than a natural extension of what went before. There are still many Pueblo communities in the Southwest, carrying on the religious, agricultural, and other practices of the Anasazi, with modern variations. And the architecture of today is very similar to that of the earlier Pueblo Period.

Meanwhile, a new Indian strain was introduced to the Southwest with the arrival of the Navajos and Apaches. Both of these tribes apparently came as migrants from northwestern Canada, where the Athapascan people lived. Residence structures have recently been discovered in the Colorado Rocky Mountains which date from about A.D. 1100 and resemble the hogan style of residence of the present-day Navajos. The Navajo people probably began to arrive in the Southwest at about the time the Pueblo culture reached its peak and shortly before the great drought; indeed, the arrival of the Navajos may have been part of the reason for the building of cliff dwellings by the Pueblo peoples as protection against attack. The Navajos, of course, expanded their influence in the Southwest, so that their culture is more dominant today than that of the older Pueblo peoples. The striking contrast between the two cultures can be seen in the juxtaposition of the Hopi reservation, with its ancient Pueblo traditions, and the surrounding larger Navajo reservation, where a completely different cultural pattern exists.

THE GREAT ARCHAEOLOGICAL SITES

There are many valuable archaeological sites throughout the Colorado Plateau, and the serious student of archaeology will want to see many of them. But for the more casual visitor, three of the ten areas recommended in this book will provide a dramatic survey of the archaeological history of the Southwest.

Canyon de Chelly National Monument, in Arizona, contains the earliest clearly identified remains in the entire plateau area, including many cliff dwellings. Set into the spectacular red canyon walls, the cliff dwellings and pictographs trace both the Basketmaker and Pueblo periods. The transition is carried right down through the modern era to the present day, since Navajo Indians continue to live and farm in the canyon. Specimens found in Mummy Cave, in the north branch of the canyon, include some items dated by tree-ring examination as far back as A.D. 348. Other ruins have been dated as recently as A.D. 1284. Excavations of the ruins in Canyon de Chelly are still in their early stages, and visitors do not have an opportunity at the present time to examine the archaeological sites.

Mesa Verde National Park, in Colorado, was a great archaeological find. Because of local Indian taboos against desecration or even habitation of houses which had been occupied by the dead, the cliff dwellings at Mesa Verde were left untouched until the end of the nineteenth century, when white men first discovered them and, unfortunately, helped themselves to some of the archaeological treasures. Many still remain, however, and a number of cliff dwellings can be visited and others inspected from a distance. The museum at Mesa Verde is the greatest single storehouse and showcase of items from the Basketmaker and Pueblo periods in the Southwest.

Bandelier National Monument, in New Mexico, completes the

span of history which begins with the early remains in Canyon de Chelly, extends through the cliff-dwelling period in Mesa Verde, and then reappears in Frijoles Canyon at Bandelier, where a number of Pueblo Indians established a settlement shortly after the abandonment of Mesa Verde. The Tyuonyi ruins at Bandelier date between 1423 and 1513 and show the remains of a great communal house, circular in form, with three small kivas built in the center court and a large kiva a few hundred yards to the east. Along the canyon wall are rooms dug into caves in the cliff, with rows of small houses built adjoining. One can walk through these ruins at Bandelier and feel much of the excitement of archaeological discovery experienced by the first scientists who inspected the place.

As one visits the Southwest, three facets of its early history stand out. These three, at least, deserve some attention and, with very little effort put into studying them, will reward the visitor richly in broadened horizons of interest and pleasure. The first and most plain to be seen, of course, is the architecture. The cliff dwellings and pueblos are not just oddities, leftovers from an ancient and outmoded way of life. On the contrary, they serve both as reminders of an indigenous talent for solving practical problems with economy and beauty and as models for today. Few architects of the modern era can exceed the simple beauty of these structures in functional design, no matter how elaborately engineered. Anyone who has visited the world-famed apartment house "Habitat," which was built for the 1967 World's Fair in Montreal as an experiment in low-cost combined modular units, will be struck by its similarity to the Pueblo structures in the Southwest.

After the architecture, for interest and beauty, comes the decorative art, both ancient and modern, the modern, of course, deriving from the ancient. Its earliest forms appear in the pictographs on the cliff faces, simple but delightful representations. Then it becomes more sophisticated and evolves from simple to more complicated designs in the black painted decorations on the pottery and in the patterns woven into the baskets. Many of these designs, particularly on the pottery, are works of art in the purest sense and are exciting for their freshness and strength.

The third facet of this early historic period worth some time and study is the range of craft abilities—the shapes of the bowls and pottery containers, the cups, the tools.

Perhaps the best way to appreciate the achievements of these early inhabitants of the Southwest who developed their own culture out of the soil is to realize how many things that we take for granted in Western culture originated with the Indians. Although not all of the items came from the Southwest, the foods, products, and recreations that follow, from a list compiled by the Mesa Verde Museum Association, were unknown in the Old World before the discovery of America in 1492.

FOODS

Corn (all varieties, including popcorn)	White potatoes	Chili peppers
	Sweet potatoes	Maple sugar
Beans (most varieties, except soy beans and black beans)	Cocoa	Peanuts
	Vanilla	Pecans
	Tapioca (manioc)	Cashews
Squashes and pumpkins	Pineapples	Black walnuts
	Strawberries	Turkeys
Tomatoes	Cranberries	Muscovy ducks

INDUSTRIAL PRODUCTS   MEDICINES

Long-staple cotton	Quinine
Rubber	Cocaine
Copal (varnish base)	Curare
Indigo and cochineal (dyes)	Cascara segrada
	Ipecac

MISCELLANEOUS PLANT ITEMS   SPORTS

Tobacco (Indians used cigars, cigarettes, pipes, snuff, and chewing tobacco)	Lacrosse
	Tobogganing
	Canoeing
Chicle (the base for chewing gum)	Snowshoeing

4
Discovery and Exploitation

In 1528, just five years after Cortez had scuttled his fleet and marched inland to claim Mexico for the Spanish Crown, the Spanish governor of that conquered land listened in fascination to stories told by an Indian slave named Tejo. The Indian reminisced about trading expeditions he had made with his father when he was a boy. He told how he and his father had gone north laden with colored feathers and how they had brought back large quantities of gold and silver from settlements which they had reached by traveling northward "between the two seas" and "across a grassy desert for forty days." Tejo described seven cities in this far-off land where riches could be found rivaling those of the City of Mexico, and where whole streets were occupied by silversmiths. His greed stimulated by this tale, the Spanish governor organized an army of 400 soldiers and 20,000 Indians and set out the following December in search of the fabled Seven Cities. He lost his way, however, and ended up on the Pacific Coast, returning to Mexico in 1531.

Meanwhile, another expedition had set forth in search of wealth in Florida, attempting to follow the earlier route of Juan Ponce de León, who had sailed from Puerto Rico in 1513 on the first of the many Spanish quests for treasure in the new world. In 1528 a Spanish force landed near Tampa, Florida, where it encountered attacks by local Indians seeking vengeance against Spanish slave traders who had been pillaging the coast for several years. The Indian attacks, combined with a series of other disasters, ultimately reduced the Spanish complement to four men, including a Moorish slave named Estevanico and a Spaniard named Alvar Nuñez Cabeza de Vaca. This foursome slowly made their way westward around the Gulf of Mexico until they reached northwestern Mexico, where they were found by Spanish slave hunters. Their stories of the Indian tribes they had encountered on their route further whetted the appetite of the Spaniards in Mexico and stimulated plans for another expedition northward.

In 1539, a small exploring party, headed by a Franciscan friar named Marcos de Niza, started north, with Estevanico as guide. Estevanico was sent to scout in advance of the main party, with instructions to send back a message in the form of a cross. If he found good country, he was to send back a cross two hands long; if rich and populous, a larger cross. Several days later, an Indian messenger returned with a cross "as tall as a man." The messenger was full of tales of seven great cities where the large houses were ornamented with turquoise. As the rest of the exploring party pressed forward, Estevanico reached the Zuñi pueblo of Hawikuh. This was undoubtedly the first time the Zuñi Indians had seen a black man, and he was a sight to behold, decked out in colored feathers, rattles, and bells. After some deliberation, however, the Indians decided that he was bad news and proceeded to kill him. Indian guides who had accompanied Estevanico hurried back to the friar and reported what had happened. Marcos erected a cross, claimed the land for Spain, and returned to Mexico full of glowing reports that the "Seven Cities of Gold" had at last been found.

His accounts were received hungrily, and the following year a major expedition was organized, under Francisco Vásquez de Coronado, to return to the northern territories, capture the cities, and take possession of their treasures. Marcos went along as a guide. In July, 1540, Coronado and an advance detachment of soldiers attacked Hawikuh. The Zuñis, having been forewarned, had assembled the warriors from all of their towns, sent their women, children, and older citizens into hiding, and were ready for a fight. Coronado led the attack and was knocked temporarily unconscious by rocks hurled from the mesa, but the town was taken after only an hour's battle.

The main body of Coronado's army arrived in September, together with women and children and a following of horses, mules, pigs, sheep, goats, and cattle. Disappointed at discovering that the Seven Cities contained no wealth but only adobe houses, the Spanish explorers turned on Marcos and sent him back to Mexico. For his part, Coronado set about sending out exploring parties from the town of Zuñi into the Pueblo country as far north as Taos, east to the buffalo plains, and west to the Hopi pueblos and the Grand Canyon. After wintering in the Pueblo villages, Coronado's army headed east. It stopped at the Indian village of Pecos, then moved northeast, then southeast. Finally, in the spring of 1542, discouraged by their lack of success in finding gold and other riches, Coronado and his army returned to Mexico. After the viceroy had heard his report, the expedition was pronounced a failure. Three Franciscan friars left behind as missionaries were promptly put to death by their intended beneficiaries. Despite the seeming futility of Coronado's expedition, it marked the first full look white men had ever had at the wonders of the Southwest.

No further interest was shown in the riches of the territory north of Mexico for forty years. Then religious zeal took hold, and a new expedition started north in the Pueblo country, this time in quest of souls to convert to Christianity. The missionaries were again put to death. In 1582 a second missionary expedition set out for the Pueblo country, returning with more encouraging reports about the land and its potential for grazing and farming. The territory was now named Nuevo Mexico, and in 1590 a preliminary attempt at colonization was made, without success. Then, in September, 1595, a wealthy mine owner, Don Juan de Oñate, offered to finance an expedition to colonize New Mexico. Three years later, an army of soldiers and settlers totaling almost

400, with an entourage of 83 carts and wagons and 7,000 head of cattle, set out from Mexico. Oñate established the first Spanish capital of the territory at a Pueblo village on the banks of the Rio Grande that was promptly renamed San Juan by the Spanish. The settling of San Juan in 1598 established the second permanent European colony in the United States, following the earlier settlement of St. Augustine, Florida, in 1565. The colonists did not fare well in their new home. Oñate's nephew and eighteen men were trapped and most of them slain on a mesa top by rebellious Indians from the Acoma pueblo. Oñate sent the murdered man's brother back with a stronger force which destroyed the mesa-top pueblo, killed the warriors, and captured some 500 women and children whom they tried and sentenced to slavery. Each of the few surviving Indian men had one foot amputated as punishment. Two Hopi Indians, who were visiting the pueblo at the time, had their right hands removed and were sent home by Oñate in this condition as a warning to others. Some years later, impoverished by the heavy costs of his expedition, Oñate was called back to Mexico to face trial on a number of charges, including his cruelty to the Indians at Acoma. He was convicted, permanently banished from New Mexico, and fined 6,000 Castilian ducats.

Despite many hardships, colonization by the Spanish continued. In 1609, they moved their capital to Santa Fe, which became a northern outpost for the Spanish authorities, serving primarily for missionary work and frontier protection. As the seventeenth century progressed, more and more missions were established in the territory, covering a wider and wider area, bracketed by Taos, Pecos, the Hopi mesas, and Zuñi. Thousands of Indians were theoretically converted to Christianity, and the Spanish religious leaders played a major role in the governing of the province. The Indians were exploited by both the missionaries and the civil authorities. Slowly but surely, resentment against the suppression of their native religion led to Indian uprisings. In 1640 the uprisings became covert, following the hanging of forty Indians who refused to abandon their ancient religious practices. The Pueblo Indians tried joining forces with their

Spanish Mission at Taos

traditional enemies, the Apaches, in hopes of ousting the Spaniards, but with little success. They were subjected to one ordeal after another, including famine, plague, and invasion by other Indians. Then a new governor arrived and decided to discourage dissension by those Indians who would not respond to Spanish missionary work by seizing forty-seven Pueblo medicine men. Three of the captives were hanged; the rest were imprisoned in Santa Fe. One of these was a medicine man named Po-pé, who had come from the pueblo which the Spaniards had renamed San Juan. Following his release from prison, embittered by the experience, Po-pé went to Taos, where he went into hiding and proceeded to organize a general rebellion among all of the Pueblo villages. The plan was to murder or expel all of the Spaniards and to destroy Santa Fe. Po-pé's plot was discovered by the Spanish governor two days before the date scheduled for the uprising, forcing the Indians to accelerate their plans in a disorganized way. Virtually all Spaniards in settlements north of Santa Fe—around 400—were murdered. Indian warriors then closed in on the capitol city and sent an envoy to the governor carrying two crosses, one white and one red. The governor was told that if he sent back the white cross, it would signal a pledge that the Spaniards would abandon the country. In this case, they would be permitted to leave in peace. If, on the other hand, the governor returned the red cross, it would signify that the Spanish would not leave, and in this case the Indians pledged to fight to the death. The red cross came back. The Indians laid siege to the city. Starvation set in. Finally, in desperation, the besieged Spaniards managed to carry out a night-time attack against the sleeping Indians, killing about 300 and driving off the rest long enough to permit escape. The Spanish, some 1,000 in all, abandoned Santa Fe and headed south. They eventually came to rest at a place called El Paso del Norte and established a settlement which today is El Paso, Texas.

The Pueblo Indians celebrated their victory over the Spaniards with an orgy of destruction. Churches were burned and torn down. Official records were destroyed. Indians who had been baptized into Christianity were washed with soapweed in the Santa Fe River to cleanse them of the stain.

The Spanish made several attempts to recapture the territory without success. Po-pé, however, flushed with his achievement, became tyrannical, destroying his opponents and generating a civil war among the Pueblo villages. At last, plague and dissension took their toll. Many of the Indians scattered in different directions, becoming sufficiently weakened that the Spaniards were able to return in 1692 and recapture Santa Fe. The Spanish never did attempt to retake the Hopi villages, which maintained an independence still evident today.

Before the Spanish came, the Indians' only beast of burden was the dog. Then Coronado arrived on horseback. The Spanish settlers who followed brought with them large numbers of horses, cattle, and sheep which they bred on the grazeland. They also developed various new forms of farming. These contributions by the Spanish brought about a revolution in the daily lives of the Indians. Following the uprising of 1680, however, Po-pé attempted to obliterate everything Spanish, in order to return the

Indians to their earlier simple existence. Many of the cattle and sheep were killed. Horses were traded to or stolen by the nomadic Indians to the north and east, thereby giving new resources to the traditional enemies of the Pueblo Indians which would come back to haunt them later in the form of raids and pillaging.

The one aspect of Po-pé's edict which his people refused to follow was the destruction of the plants which the Spanish had introduced, especially the peach trees. The Indians contended that the plants had a divine spark and could not be eliminated.

After the year 1692, and following the reconquest of New Mexico by the Spanish in that year, the colonists lived in relative peace with the Indians for a century. Spanish settlements continued to grow. Crops and cattle flourished within the limits imposed by nature. Trade began to expand. The villages of Taos and Pecos were designated as principal trading posts, while Santa Fe became the major focal point for expeditions between the territory and Mexico to the south, being the northern termination of the main route, called the Camino Real—the Royal Road.

Meanwhile, Spain's foreign affairs were beginning to have an impact on the new territory. France's disputes with Spain caused a prohibition against trading between the Spanish colonists in New Mexico and the French in Louisiana early in the eighteenth century. Then, as the French and Indian War came to an end, France ceded to Spain all of Louisiana west of the Mississippi River, and the French peril ceased to exist. Fur traders from French Canada arrived in Santa Fe in 1739, marking the beginning of a new era. The traders opened up the first link between the Southwest and the North and East and carried back information about the glittering possibilities of the Southwestern territory. The Spanish themselves were broadening their reach into California to join the missions in the Southwest with those on the Pacific coast. Along the route, Spanish missionaries began exploring the area eventually to become Utah, which had been avoided by colonists because of its forbidding appearance.

At the same time, attentions began turning to the east. Expeditions were sent out from Santa Fe to establish a route to St. Louis in 1792, marking the start of what was to become famous

as the Santa Fe Trail. In 1803, President Thomas Jefferson, to
the consternation of many who thought him foolhardy, paid
$15 million to Napoleon—the near bankrupt emperor of France
—to purchase the Louisiana territory. An exploratory expedition
was sent out from Washington into the new territory under the
leadership of a young army lieutenant named Zebulon M. Pike.
Pike reached the present site of Pueblo, Colorado, in November,
1806. He set out from there with a handful of men to scale the
great mountain peak looming in the distance but was turned
back by a blizzard. Nonetheless, his effort was memorialized for
posterity by the naming of the peak in his honor. Lieutenant Pike
went on to cross the Sangre de Cristo Mountains into the San
Luis Valley beyond, heading toward the Rio Grande and the
Spanish territory. The Spanish officials, alarmed by the westward
expansion of the United States government and fearing an invasion of American pioneers, reacted violently when they learned
that Lieutenant Pike had constructed a stockade on the opposite
bank of the Rio Grande and had raised the American flag there.
A contingent of Spanish soldiers was sent out. Pike and his men
were arrested and taken in chains to Santa Fe; from there they
were escorted to the Louisiana frontier and released, taking back
with them the first authentic official information about the
Southwest.

After Mexico won independence from Spain in 1821, the
policy of the civil government in the New Mexico territory
toward outsiders changed from hostility to a more welcoming
attitude. In 1822, the first wagon train of goods from Missouri
crossed the plains to Santa Fe and opened up that trading route.
Two years later, a still more ambitious expedition traveled the
Santa Fe Trail, converting a $30,000 investment in Eastern goods
into $180,000 in gold and silver plus $10,000 worth of furs.

Fur trading played an important role in the opening of the
Southwest. Furs were acquired by trading with the Indians or
by trapping and were ultimately sold mainly in Europe, where
goods were obtained in return. The fur business depended
largely on credit because of the long interval before pelts could
be converted into trading goods and cash. In the Rockies, the

unit of value at trading posts became the beaver skin.

As the Santa Fe Trail was opened up between Missouri and Santa Fe to bring in manufactured goods in exchange for furs and silver, a second trading route, which came to be known as the Old Spanish Trail, was opened up between Santa Fe, Taos, and Los Angeles. It was blazed by a fur-trading party in 1830. With the passage of time, this route was used by horse traders and later by California-bound emigrants during the gold rush. All of this lively activity brought with it vigorous growth and an optimistic outlook. In 1834, the first newspaper in the Southwest was published in Santa Fe, later moving to Taos. It was grandly named *El Crepúsculo de la Libertad* (The Dawn of Liberty).

In 1846, President Polk declared that a state of war existed between the United States and Mexico. Plans were laid for the invasion of New Mexico and California by the Army of the West, under the command of Colonel Stephen W. Kearny. Kearny and his army marched on Santa Fe in August of that year. They met with no opposition from the local residents but instead received a thirteen-gun salute. Kearny's force included five companies of untrained Mormon recruits—the Mormon Battalion—organized in Council Bluffs, Iowa. Although they did no fighting, the men of the Mormon Battalion gained considerable experience and toughening as they followed Kearny across the Southwest and opened up a wagon road from Santa Fe to the Pacific. This experience was to serve the Mormons well as they moved on into the territory destined to become the State of Utah.

The Mexican War resulted in the Treaty of Guadalupe in 1848, under which the Southwest territory was ceded to the United States. In 1847, while the Mexican War was still in progress, 12,000 Mormons migrated to their new Zion near the Great Salt Lake. Bigotry and oppression had hounded them all across the continent wherever they had sought to settle. Driven by an unparalleled zeal, in the face of all adversity, their aim now was to move far away—out into unsettled territory—and establish a new community in peace. They scratched their new settlement in the middle of the plains and sent emissaries south into the

Colorado Plateau, where they created farms and small settlements, many of which exist even today.

It was late in the summer of 1847 when the Mormons arrived in the Utah territory, but the colonists set to work immediately and planted several thousand acres of wheat and corn. In the spring of 1848 the crops seemed to be coming along well. Then came an untimely frost on June 4, 1848, which destroyed most of the crops. The frost was followed by an invasion of crickets which blackened the land and threatened to finish off what remained. Then a miracle occurred. Close behind the crickets came flocks of gulls, hundreds of them, many miles from their seacoast homes, who descended on the crickets and disposed of them in short order. The "miracle of the gulls" has become a cherished item of folklore for the Mormon people, a symbol of divine intervention against adversity.

Following the traders and the Mormon settlers came the miners to the Southwest. The cry of "Gold!" went out from the Colorado territory in 1859. By the end of that summer, 100,000 prospectors had jammed the area surrounding what is now Denver. While half of these emigrants returned east, thousands of others ranged throughout the area, establishing settlements and staking out claims. A smaller gold rush hit Arizona in 1862, bringing a stampede into that area destined to become Tucson. A large criminal population accompanied the gold rush, generating a demand on Congress to create the territory of Arizona, which was done in February of 1863, in order to establish orderly government there.

All of these incursions into the Southwest country had a disastrous impact on the Indians, who had been living their own life there without interference, except from the Spanish, for many centuries. Now the settlers were taking the land, killing the buffaloes, and committing atrocities on the Indians themselves. Symbolizing the attitude of many whites toward the new territory was the hunting trip organized in 1855 by an Irish baronet, Sir George Gore. Sir George was one of a growing number of Europeans who were taken by the romance and excitement of the wild West and who could afford a trip of this kind—a sort of American safari, an improbable fashion of the times. Sir George was accompanied by a coterie of 40 servants, 14 dogs, 112 horses, 6 wagons, 21 carts, and 12 yoke of oxen, while engaging in the slaughter of some 3,000 buffaloes, 40 grizzly bears, and countless deer and antelopes. The Indians, troubled by the wanton destruction of their food supply, were sorely tempted to attack Gore and his party but held back. (It is said that Gore, while hunting game in Colorado, came upon gold and exclaimed, "I did not come here to seek gold! I don't need it. This is a pleasure hunt." He broke camp immediately to avoid the risk of desertion by his men.)

The Mormons had a number of scrapes with the Indians as they established their far-flung settlements in Utah. In 1849 a group of settlers set up a colony on the Provo River near a favorite Ute fishing ground. The Mormons made promises that they would not interfere with the Indians' use of the land or the river and were permitted, in turn, to start farming and building homes without restraint. Then, toward the end of summer, the peace was shattered by the killing of an Indian in a dispute over a shirt. Brigham Young had at first refused to help the settlers, but as relations with the Indians worsened he sent two companies of militia from Salt Lake City. An attempt at peaceful settlement failed when a band of warriors opened fire during a parley. Fierce fighting ensued, during which one white man and a number of Indians were killed.

When Mormon settlers established a farming community at Moab in 1855, an early period of good will came to an end with a sudden series of attacks by the Indians, who killed three of the settlers and set a number of fires. The morning following the attacks the Mormons abandoned their settlement, departing so hurriedly that they left water coursing through a freshly dug irrigation canal. The water continued to run for several years and eventually carved out a 25-foot arroyo.

The most serious but final conflict between the Utes and the Mormons, the Black Hawk War, took place between 1865 and 1868. When it ended, more than fifty Mormons had died, large numbers of livestock had been destroyed, and a number of settlements had been abandoned. The war ultimately petered out, and the Utes agreed to settle on a reservation.

Among the Pueblo Indians, there was little fighting with the whites, except for a brief uprising at Taos in 1847, stirred up by the Mexicans, with the aid of firewater, in an effort to expel the Americans. After the Mexican War had ended in 1849, new arrivals from the East robbed and pillaged the Pueblo villages, but the Indians maintained a stout patience throughout most of these outrages.

The nearby Navajos also appeared to be peaceful for a while. Navajo raids had occurred frequently in the Southwest, even during the Spanish settlement, but a period of calm ensued after the construction of Fort Defiance in Navajo country in 1851. Then, one day in 1858, an army officer's slave got into a fight with a Navajo subchief, leading to a Navajo attack on the fort and a resumption of raids on various settlements. The Civil War prevented extensive military expeditions against the Navajos, but finally, in the winter of 1863–1864, the raids had increased to such an extent that Colonel Kit Carson was sent out by the War Department to round up the Navajos. He took a large force into the Navajo stronghold at Canyon de Chelly, with the intent of destroying the Navajos' food supply, thereby forcing them from their hideouts. Carson's soldiers cut down more than 2,000 peach trees and destroyed flocks, herds, and crops. Most of the Navajos surrendered as starvation closed in. They were marched to Bosque Redondo, near Fort Sumner, New Mexico, where they were to be trained in farming. After four years of misery and starvation in alien country, the Navajos were allowed by treaty to return to their homes and establish a permanent reservation. They were supplied with sheep and goats in an effort to encourage pastoral pursuits.

Military expeditions continued against the adjoining tribes of Apaches and Comanches, but comparative Indian peace reigned in the Southwest thereafter, with the exception of a final desperate uprising by the Ute Indians in southwestern Colorado in 1875, protesting the invasion of reservation lands by prospectors. Mightily provoked, the Utes finally responded to abuse by an

Indian agent. Their brief uprising resulted in their being forced to give up most of their land holdings in Colorado.

As in other parts of the country, the conflict between Indians and settlers in the Southwest was marked by much misunderstanding and treachery on both sides. White men committed outrages which were inexcusable, and by the same token Indians perpetrated raids and slaughter which destroyed many innocent people. In the end, the Indians were segregated on lands which were generally bleak and unproductive. A benign government played a caretaker role which might have destroyed less enterprising peoples, but on the whole the Indians of the Southwest have flourished, so much so that the Navajo tribe has increased many times. New riches provided by nature, with the discovery of oil and uranium on Indian lands, have provided an ironic form of compensation for many of the wrongs imposed during reservation life.

A kaleidoscopic view of the Southwest's history can be seen in the community of Taos, New Mexico. Today a tourist center, spoiled by gas stations and neon signs, it has witnessed, over the last four centuries, many of the forces which have shaped the development of the entire Colorado Plateau area. The Indian pueblo at Taos was first discovered in 1540 by Hernando de Alvarado during the Coronado expedition. Spanish colonists settled at Taos when Oñate began to colonize the territory, receiving a friendly welcome from the Indians. As the years wore on, however, the Indians grew alarmed at the increasing number of Spanish settlers and of intermarriages between the two races. An Indian council requested that the Spaniards move "a league away," resulting in the establishment of two separate villages, one Indian, one Spanish. The two communities continued to provide joint protection for each other against attacks by roving Indian bands. A Franciscan friar started the process of Christianizing the Indians with the construction of a church in 1620, near the pueblo. In 1631 he was put to death by the Indians, who were becoming increasingly resentful of the white man's imposition of an alien religion. By 1650, bad blood had increased to such an extent that Taos became the center for planning an uprising against the Spanish which did not succeed. A generation later, however, the Indian leader Po-pé, after being released from Spanish confinement, made his headquarters in the Taos pueblo, from which he planned and organized the revolt which resulted in the expulsion of the Spanish from the entire territory. When De Vargas reconquered Santa Fe in 1692, he continued his march up to Taos and re-established a Spanish settlement there.

Trouble with roving Comanche bands continued from time to time. In 1760, Indians attacked the town and carried away fifty women and children. Spanish soldiers organized an expedition and massacred four hundred Indians in reprisal. Eventually, Taos became a major trading center. During the eighteenth century, the annual Taos fair brought Indians, Spanish traders, and settlers there from all over the Southwest to exchange goods and gossip. In time, Taos became the busiest settlement in the territory. Trappers adopted Taos as a trading base. During the Mexican War, the Spanish recruited Indians to fight off the Americans who had come to town in large numbers, but the effort was quickly dissipated. Taos became a trading post for gold prospectors in the 1860's. Its history and its beauty made it a magnet for artists and writers toward the end of the nineteenth century, and by the early part of the twentieth it was established as an art colony and, ultimately, as a major tourist attraction. Much of the old Spanish town can still be seen, as well as the Indian pueblo. If you let your imagination go, you can still hear the hoofbeats of Indian horses and the voices of Spanish missionaries above the transistor radios and the roar of tourist buses.

The other major Pueblo Indian trading post, Pecos, did not fare so well. It was the easternmost inhabited village at the time of the Spanish conquest and was visited by Coronado during his 1540 expedition. The land was good, water was plentiful, and the situation was excellent for trading purposes. The Indians kept Pecos to themselves until 1583, when the Spanish made a second visit, following up with a full-fledged attack in 1590. In 1598 it became a Spanish mission. The people of Pecos participated in the 1680 rebellion which drove the Spanish back to the border.

They had suffered less from the Spaniards than had those of many other Indian villages, but their fate at the hands of enemy Indian tribes was less propitious. Apache and Comanche raids had sadly reduced their warrior population. Finally, in 1750, the town fathers decided to send forth a military expedition against the enemy. All but one warrior in the ill-fated Pecos force were killed in a Comanche ambush. Thereafter a smallpox epidemic hit the village, leaving only 180 survivors. Then came mountain fever, a form of typhoid, and at last the village was abandoned in 1838 when the final 17 survivors moved out. The pueblo fell into ruins, speeded on its way by vandals seeking timbers for beams and firewood.

The Indians have another explanation for the fall of Pecos. The ancient deity of the Pueblo was a snake god. In honor of the deity, a large snake was kept alive in the kiva, where it received regular offerings. A sacred fire was tended on the kiva altar. When the Indians became converted to Christianity, fewer and fewer practiced their traditional religion. The fire was neglected and went out. Then came the epidemic which resulted in the death of most of the small children of the Pueblo. Seeing this, the villagers decided that a human sacrifice to the snake god would have to be made. The son of the principal warrior was chosen for the sacrifice. Having only one son left, the warrior asked the priest to hide his son and substitute a young goat. The snake was not deceived by the substitution, however, and concluded that his people had truly abandoned their old religion. He crawled out of the kiva and quietly disappeared into the Rio Grande River. With the ancient deity gone, the end was inevitable.

5
The Wild and Woolly West

In 1885, in St. Louis, Missouri, artist Cessily Adams hired a group of Sioux Indians to pose for an oversized canvas depicting "Custer's Last Fight." The local art galleries showed little interest in the painting of Little Big Horn, but finally it was sold to a saloon near Eighth and Olive Streets to hang behind the bar. Not long thereafter, the saloon's proprietor found himself in financial difficulties, and the painting was handed over to the Anheuser-Busch Brewing Company in partial settlement for what the proprietor owed on beer deliveries. The painting gathered dust at the brewery for a while, until a public relations man suggested that the company make lithographic reproductions of the painting to send to its customers as a good-will promotion item. The lithographs were enthusiastically received, and before long 10,000 copies of the painting of the bloody battle were hanging in as many drinking establishments across the country.

There are those who claim that debating among bar patrons over Adams's picture of "Custer's Last Fight" was a major factor in generating interest in Western lore and history. But others were also busy stirring up interest in the wild West. Frederic Remington, the artist and sculptor, was one; Ned Buntline, Prentiss Ingraham, and Edward L. Wheeler together wrote hundreds of dime novels about adventures on the plains and in the mountains of the West; and Buffalo Bill Cody organized the first successful traveling Wild West Show.

The story of William F. Cody's first performance is quite a tale unto itself. After some years as a military scout and buffalo hunter for the railroad, during which he won the nickname "Buffalo" Bill because of the great numbers of buffaloes he shot and supplied to the company, Cody, with retirement in mind, bought a ranch in North Platte, Nebraska, which he called "Welcome Wigwam." Shortly thereafter, when the local city officials were making plans to celebrate the Fourth of July, they asked Cody to organize the celebration. He agreed to take on the job and decided to recreate the spirit of the West, complete with a stage holdup, buffalo chase, sharpshooting, soldiers and Indians, and plenty of hard-riding horses. The Fourth of July performance was wildly successful, so successful, in fact, that during the stage holdup the soldier and Indian actors, who were truly soldiers and Indians, generated such an air of authenticity that the horses pulling the stagecoach bolted out of control. The stage's passengers included various high officials, led by the mayor. After a mad scene with much distress on the part of the officials, the runaway stagecoach was at last brought under control and ruffled official tempers soothed. By the time the show was over, all agreed that it had been a spectacular beginning and should be carried on. After some replanning to ensure that future acts would be kept under somewhat better restraint, Cody put the show on the road as "The Wild West Rocky Mountain and Prairie Expedition." In time, Buffalo Bill's Wild West Show played throughout the United States and Europe, including a command performance for Queen Victoria. Interest in the excitement of the West was now secure.

With the passage of years, stories about the old West improved with telling, until myth and fact became inseparable. Taking for granted a little tongue in cheek, the stories of the West and the Southwest are fascinating and well worth repeating.

THE TRAPPERS

Following the Spanish, the first of the hearty breed of adventurers to enter the Southwest in any numbers were the trappers, who came seeking their fortunes in animal skins. Although there were many fur-bearing animals in the West, the beaver was the most highly prized from many points of view. The price for beaver fur in St. Louis ranged between $4 and $6 per pound. Each beaver pelt weighed between one and a half and two pounds. Beavers were found primarily living in burrows along the banks of streams and waterways lined with trees, which provided them with food and building materials.

Trappers usually worked in groups, although a few preferred to work alone. Each trapper usually carried between four and six iron traps, each trap weighing about five pounds. The traps were set out in the early evening and then collected the following dawn. The customary procedure was to bait a leaf overhanging the water near the entrance to a beaver burrow with the secretion from a beaver's castor gland and then place a trap in the water below the leaf at a depth of about four inches. The leaf's appealing scent attracted the beaver, who, in his effort to reach it, usually stood up on his hind legs and walked into the water —and the trap. The weight of the trap then caused the beaver to drown before he could gnaw off the leg imprisoned by the spring.

A mature beaver weighed between thirty and forty pounds and therefore was usually skinned on the spot. A slit was cut down the belly and four crosswise cuts made down the insides of the legs. The pelt was then removed, stretched on a frame, scraped, and dried. It was then folded, fur side in, for carrying. Many trappers removed the beaver's tail, which was regarded as a delicacy, and the castor glands for baiting other traps. A successful trapper could gather as much as $15 to $30 a day in beaver pelts while he was in the field.

Trapping companies were organized to purchase furs on the site and then transport them to market. In time, an annual rendezvous was organized for trappers to bring in the year's take and purchase supplies for the following year. The rendezvous also served as a time for socializing, games, and high living.

Some trappers worked in the mountains, earning the appellation "mountain men," and were the original sources of many tall tales about their endurance and their capacity for hard liquor. They preferred living alone in the wilds but occasionally emerged to spend their earnings riotously over the course of two or three days. They learned to use many of the skills of the Indians. They also often wore decorative beads and feathers and had Indian wives. The fur traders acquired their skins either by trading directly with the Indians or by dealing with these mountain men, some of whom worked on salary, others as independent entrepreneurs.

Among the colorful early trappers and traders operating out of Santa Fe were Sylvester Pattie and his son, James Ohio Pattie. For ten years beginning in 1824, father and son and then son alone ranged throughout the Southwest, trading, trapping, and meeting with many adventures. In 1828 the two were imprisoned in San Diego. The father died there, but the son managed to get himself released, reportedly because he carried a quantity of smallpox vaccine with which he vaccinated some 22,000 persons in exchange for his freedom. Another famous trapper-adventurer, who made a small fortune in his early days as a mountain man and later as a partner in the Rocky Mountain Fur Company, was Jedediah S. Smith. Smith conducted a number of explorations through Utah, discovering new routes into California and back. In 1831 his pistols mysteriously turned up for sale at the trading post in Taos. After inquiry it developed that Smith had met up with a group of Comanche youths along the Cimarron cutoff from the Santa Fe Trail. They had fallen into trading jokes with him, all the while maneuvering mirrors which hung in their hair to blind Smith's horse, causing it to rear. As he tried to bring his horse under control, they ran him through with their lances. Such was the peril of life in the Southwest, even for fabled heroes.

Another renowned mountain man was Hugh Glass, who was once torn by a grizzly bear. He was left to die by two companions who had been assigned to look after him while the rest of the trapping party went on its way. The two watchmen rejoined the party a few days later, carrying Glass's gun and knife and graphically describing his death and burial. Glass actually had not died but had lain in a coma, while his two fellow trappers divided up his property and abandoned him to a fate they assumed was inevitable. Inch by inch he crawled to a spring for water and found sustenance from a bush of wild cherries overhead. With only his razor as a weapon, he traveled hundreds of miles through hostile territory, living mainly off buffalo calves, until finally he met another party of trappers. Eventually, he rejoined his original party and vented his views —with some restraint, considering his grievance—against those who had abandoned him.

And then there was "Uncle Dick" Wootton, who managed to find considerable financial success through skill and daring. Richens Lacy Wootton was born in Virginia in 1816, worked first on a tobacco plantation, then in a cotton field, and finally wandered to Independence, Missouri, the starting point for caravans heading out on the Santa Fe Trail. His head filled with stories about the West, and dazzled by the wealth that could be made from trapping beaver furs, young Wootton wound up in Colorado as a trapper. He went out on a number of lengthy trapping expeditions filled with adventure and mishap and finally, having gathered a modest sum for his efforts, turned to raising buffaloes on a farm. Along the way he had escaped murder at the hands of the Ute Indians, fought his way out of a canyon, confronted hungry wolves, and spent several hours treed by a grizzly.

Wootton led a party of volunteers to help put down the revolution at Taos. He also led a posse after a band of Indians who had massacred stagecoach passengers along the Santa Fe Trail, using circling ravens as his guide to the Indians' camp.

When Uncle Dick Wootton learned that he could sell sheep in California at ten times their price in New Mexico, he invested in 9,000 head. With only four assistants, a shepherd dog, and eight trained goats as guides, he successfully maneuvered the journey with the loss of only 100 sheep, turning a huge profit in the process. Along the way, the Ute Indians attacked him. Wootton countered by grabbing their chief, Uncotash, around the waist, pulling him to the ground, and then sitting astraddle the chief's stomach with a knife to his ribs until the Indians agreed to leave him alone.

On another occasion, Uncle Dick Wootton teamed up with Tom Tobin to hunt the bandit Espinosa and a companion, on whose heads bounties had been placed. After a hard chase and tough resistance, the bandits were killed. Tobin cut off their heads and carried them back to Santa Fe in a bag to prove the deed and collect the reward.

Around this time, Wootton was invited to visit the home of Brigham Young in Salt Lake City. He had to cross a number of streams on his way to the city. Each time his buckskin trousers got wet they stretched, and Wootton was forced to cut strips off the bottom so they would not drag on the ground. When he finally reached the dry desert in Utah, the hot sun shrank his trousers so that they came up above his knees. His arrival in Salt Lake City was greeted with broad smiles.

Wootton set up a trading operation in Pueblo, Colorado, to deal with emigrants heading for the Southwest. His stock in trade was fresh oxen, which he traded for weary animals, exhausted from the trek overland. His usual terms were three or four tired beasts for one fresh one. He sent the exhausted oxen to a nearby ranch, where they pastured for a few weeks and then came back to be exchanged for other tired animals who had just arrived in town. The ratio was obviously very favorable, and, as Wootton conceded, "in this way I increased my herd very rapidly."

Pueblo suffered a bitter experience in 1854 at the hands of the Ute Indians. Wootton had noticed that the Utes were acting suspiciously and cautioned his neighbors not to permit them into the fort. On Christmas Day, however, liquor flowed freely, and heedless of Wootton's warning the Mexicans guarding the fort invited the Indians in to have a drink. Once inside the fort, the Indians turned on their hosts and massacred all but a young Mexican girl, two children, and one man who had a bullet put through his tongue but was later able to recount what had happened by using sign language. Thereafter, the mountain men stopped using Pueblo as a rendezvous because of a rumor that the community was haunted by headless Mexican women.

As Uncle Dick Wootton became more ambitious, he organized a freight run with a train nearly a mile long, comprising thirty-six prairie schooners with five pairs of oxen each, to ply the Santa Fe Trail. The train moved 16 miles a day, and each round trip produced a profit of $10,000. Later he organized a stagecoach run, covering the distance from Santa Fe to Independence, Missouri, in only fourteen days, at a fare of $250 per person. The stagecoach ran nonstop, not even making rest stops at night.

Wootton's most renowned business venture, however, was the toll road he constructed over Raton Pass, following an old Indian trail, which became part of the Santa Fe Trail, replacing the Cimarron branch of the trail, which crossed the desert and was considered dangerous. This private toll road, completed in 1865, provided a handsome income for Wootton. His fee was $1.50 per wagon, with lower rates for people traveling on horse or on foot. He permitted Indians to pass free, largely to avoid trouble, but charged Mexicans and others, which caused a great deal of protest. When the railroad was finally built, Wootton closed down the toll road and retired. In the meantime, he had made many trips to the bank with whiskey kegs full of silver dollars.

A mountain man who lived and died at his trade was Old Bill Williams, regarded as one of the most eccentric characters in the Southwest. Born in North Carolina and raised in Missouri, he began his career as an itinerant preacher, settling among the Osage Indians in Missouri. His attempts to convert the Indians to Christianity backfired, however, and he ended up accepting their religious beliefs instead and was adopted into the tribe. Williams married an Indian girl who produced two daughters for him. When his wife died, Williams left the tribe and went off to become a trapper, hunter, and guide. He trapped alone, usually carrying six traps plus his rifle, a blanket, and his razor-sharp knife. He would return from an expedition after a few weeks, staggering under a load of pelts. He would sell these immediately and then drink up his profits in Taos until his money was gone. Once he traded a stack of pelts for a barrel of whiskey, knocked the top off the barrel, issued an open invitation to anyone and everyone to join him, and proceeded, with a fair amount of help, to drain the barrel dry.

Williams apparently was an awesome sight, tall and bony, long-haired, and always clad in buckskin shirt and trousers. When he visited a daughter living near St. Louis, his grandchild screamed at the sight of him and went to hide under the bed.

Williams's one attempt at commercial enterprise was short-lived. He set up a dry goods store in Taos but soon became impatient with the haggling by his female customers over prices and, in a fit of temper, threw bolt after bolt of yard goods down the main street, enjoying himself as he watched the women scramble for the calico. He then packed up his traps and headed back into the mountains.

Williams's weakness for liquor was his undoing. His friendship with the Ute Indians had led to his adoption into that tribe and then to his being entrusted with a quantity of furs to be sold for the Utes in Taos. After he had sold the furs, Williams went to satisfy his thirst in a nearby saloon and continued the spree until he had spent all of the proceeds. Fearing to return to the mountains without the Utes' money, he signed on as a guide to a military expedition which was going out against a band of Apaches. The expedition followed the Apaches to Cumbres Pass, where the Apaches were joined by Utes in a pitched battle against the troops, during which thirty-six Indians were killed. Williams suffered a wound in his arm and took refuge while it healed. Next he signed on as a guide for John C. Frémont, who had gained fame for his topographic mapping of the west. Frémont, in 1848, was setting out on a trip to map a possible railroad route. Uncle Dick Wootton had been selected as Frémont's guide but later quit when Frémont said he wanted to go into snow country. After also failing to hire Kit Carson, Frémont settled on Old Bill Williams. After the party was underway, Williams urged Frémont to travel one route while Frémont insisted on another and sent Old Bill to the rear. The expedition was met by snow and ice, and eleven men froze to death. Old Bill avoided starvation by capturing a deer. He cut out the liver and ate it raw and then tore off great mouthfuls of raw flesh "like a savage animal." Two months after arriving back in Taos, Williams set out again with Frémont to recover the goods and money which Frémont had concealed in the mountains. As they made camp one evening and sat by the campfire smoking, a group of Utes, seeking vengeance for a recent murderous foray by a troop of soldiers, came upon them by surprise. Both men were killed. Williams, who had accepted a belief in transmigration when he was adopted by the Utes, had prophesied that he would be reincarnated as a buck elk. For several years after his death, a number of plainsmen refused to kill buck elks for fear of killing their old friend by mistake.

Another of the mountain men who gained wide repute was Christopher (Kit) Carson. Born in Kentucky in 1809, he spent his boyhood in Missouri, where, as a saddler's apprentice, he first heard exciting tales of the life of trappers and traders. In 1826, at the age of seventeen, he joined a caravan en route to Santa Fe. From there he went to Taos, where he served as saddler, wrangler, cook, teamster, and trapper. Carson married an Arapaho Indian girl, who died shortly after childbirth. His second marriage, to a Cheyenne, ended when she chased him out of their cabin and threw his belongings out after him. His third marriage, to a Spanish girl from a wealthy family, produced eight children and extensive land holdings. Carson became the Indian agent at Taos and then a colonel in the Union Army. After the Civil War, he was reappointed Indian agent and selected to mediate with the tribes of the Southwest. One of his tasks was to end the constant marauding by the Navajos, which he accomplished by driving them from their home in Canyon de Chelly (see Chapter 6).

The trappers' reputation as hard-drinking, gun-slinging men was widespread and often took the form of humorous tales. One story is told of a coroner who delivered a verdict on the cause of death of a cowboy who had been shot by a trapper during a whiskey-soaked argument. The dispute had centered on whether wildcats have long tails. The coroner's formal decision was that anyone crazy enough to call a whiskey-drinking trapper a *liar* had "died of ignorance."

Tall tales of wild animals in the Southwest were also widespread, as witness this verbatim story told by an old-timer.

I caught a bear onct.

This here bear got so tame I used to ride him after cattle. Only just two things was wrong with him. He et too much and he had one ear off. I called him Herkimer.

One day me and Herkimer was out for some yearlings, and we run smack into another bear. My outfit growls, the other bear growls, and first thing I know me and Herkimer light right on top of that other bear. I yell, I throw rocks, and I can't get that outfit split—and what's more, Herkimer ain't doing so well. I get me a club and by banging both of them get the outfit squared off long enough to climb on Herkimer and make tracks with that wild bear about six feet behind. The wild one ain't got no rider to carry and he gains on us, growling like all hell. I sock in my spurs and grab Herkimer's ear—and then by gad I notice I'm hanging onto that outfit with both hands—and I got me an ear in each hand. . . .

THE PROSPECTORS

Fringing the Southwest are a number of mining areas which have produced fortunes in gold, silver, copper, and uranium. These areas have also produced countless rags-to-riches stories and many myths of lost mines which still generate fevered searches by the ever-hopeful looking for their fortunes at the end of a shovel.

The first gold rush in the Southwest came in 1859, ten years after the great gold rush in California. News of a small discovery of gold near Pike's Peak, west of Denver, led to an influx of hundreds of thousands of fortune seekers, many traveling in prairie schooners painted with signs "Pike's Peak or Bust." Many were busted.

One of the Pike's Peak fortune seekers was H. A. W. Tabor, a Vermont-born stonecutter who had come to Colorado early in

1859 with his wife and small son. He moved from field to field, following each new strike, enduring years of hardship and privation. He found several thousand dollars' worth of gold dust, but his claim was soon exhausted, and he and his family moved to Buckskin Joe, where they took in boarders to keep the family fed. Then, in 1878, a new group of fortune seekers, reworking the old claims, discovered carbonate of lead, with a high silver content, in the heavy red sands which had been cast aside in the gold sluicing operations. The discovery of silver brought in new hordes of prospectors. Tabor, who had learned his lesson, stuck to storekeeping and serving as postmaster. One day two German shoemakers came into his store and asked to be supplied with the necessities for prospecting. Tabor grubstaked them in return for a promise of one third of their discoveries. As the story goes, the two men quietly helped themselves to a jug of whiskey behind Tabor's back and fortified themselves before starting off on their prospecting. Only a mile out of camp they climbed a hill and set to work digging in the shade of a pine tree. Almost immediately they struck a silver lode at the only point on the hill where the vein came anywhere near the surface. Tabor's $17 grubstake produced $500,000 in dividends from the Little Pittsburg Mine. He sold out the rest of his interest for $1 million. Some sharp promoters set out to fleece Tabor of his newly won fortune by selling him a mine shaft in which silver ore had been carefully salted to give the appearance of discovery. Tabor, to the delight of those who had taken him, sent men into the shaft to work the mine. They promptly hit the Chrysolite lode, one of the great discoveries in the district. Tabor continued to make lucky investments, finally topping them off with the Matchless Mine. Then, with a fortune estimated at more than $9 million, Tabor turned to a public career. He was elected mayor of Leadville, then lieutenant-governor of Colorado. He presented Leadville with a fire department, financed military companies, and built various business structures and opera houses.

Tabor built one opera house in Leadville with private boxes for the use of himself and a friendly business associate, Bill Bush. One evening, when Gladys Robeson, a popular actress of the day, appeared on stage in red tights, Tabor tossed a handful of silver dollars onto the stage. Bush countered by tossing two handfuls, then Tabor, four. Both men sent to the gambling rooms for bags of gold pieces, which they proceeded to cascade in increasing numbers upon the lucky lady, with the encouragement of the shouting audience, which also began to participate. By the time the shower of coins had ended, the actress had collected almost $5,000, with the stagehands helping themselves to a goodly sum as well. At the end of it all, independent lady that she was, Miss Robeson politely refused to be introduced to either Tabor or Bush.

Wealth sometimes begets vanity. When Tabor built the Tabor Grand Opera House in Denver, he was surprised one day to see a portrait of a stranger in the main lobby. "Who's that?" he asked. "William Shakespeare," was the reply. "Who's he?" asked Tabor. "The greatest playwright in history," came the answer. "What the hell did he ever do for Colorado?" demanded Tabor. "Put my picture up there." And they did.

Another wealthy miner whose vanity took a different turn was Winfield Scott Stratton, an ex-carpenter. Stratton attended a party at the Brown Palace Hotel in Denver and started throwing champagne bottles over the railing onto the lobby floor below. The manager took offense at this behavior and told him, "Get out of my hotel." The next day, Stratton bought the Brown Palace for $1 million cash, then went back and told the manager, "Now you get out of *my* hotel."

H. A. W. Tabor divorced his first wife and married the beautiful divorcee, "Baby" Doe, at a lavish wedding in Washington, D.C., attended by President Chester A. Arthur. With the collapse of silver prices in the panic of 1893, Tabor's empire fell and he was rendered virtually penniless. He returned to the job of postmaster, which he held until his death in 1899. His last instructions to Baby Doe were "Hold on to the Matchless." Doggedly, his widow followed Tabor's instructions, living alone in a rough shack beside the mine shaft until her own death in 1935.

Adjoining the Matchless Mine to the south was an undeveloped claim purchased in 1879 by Jim Baxter, who sank a hundred-foot shaft but, finding no ore, sold out for $30,000. On the very next morning, the new owners fired off a single charge of dynamite, exposing a vein of almost pure silver. More than half a million dollars was taken out within three months. In one twenty-four hour period $118,500 worth of silver was mined. Similar stories of quick riches abound throughout the Southwest.

At Cripple Creek, a cowboy named Bob Womack found a strike of gold, then proceeded to get drunk and sell it for $500.

Two druggists from Colorado Springs, with no knowledge of mining or geology, simply threw a hat into the air and dug where it fell, discovering a mine they later called "The Pharmacist."

The proprietors of a grocery store accepted a 50 percent interest in a claim in payment of a $36.40 grocery bill, then sold it to a schoolteacher who struck a vein of gold on the claim and made $13 million.

In 1877, Ed Schieffelin set off into Apache country to look for gold. He was warned by a fellow soldier, "Instead of a mine, you'll find a tombstone." When he finally came upon some rich-looking ore, Schieffelin staked out a claim which he called "Tombstone," the name later adopted by the Arizona city which sprang up nearby. Then his brother joined Schieffelin prospecting and together they found a still richer lode. His brother commented, "You're a lucky cuss," and the Lucky Cuss Mine it became, one of the richest mines in Arizona.

Among the liveliest gold-mining towns in southwestern Colorado was Telluride, which retains to this day the air of an affluent frontier community. The celebrated Smuggler Mine was struck on a lapsed claim here, causing a rush of prospectors who pitted the surrounding mountainsides with holes. At the peak of its boom, Telluride had a population of 5,000 and an elegant opera house which still stands.

The constant companion of prospectors in the Southwest was the burro, a long-eared creature often called the "Arizona nightingale" because of its unusual bray. Burros were first introduced to the Southwest by the Spaniards. Missionaries found the little animals useful for exploring, because of their toughness and ability to get along with little food and water, subsisting on grass and bark. There are those who claim that a burro can do as well as a prospector at discovering ore. A story is told of Henry Wickenburg, who pursued his wandering burro into the hills. The burro, enjoying his freedom, eluded every effort at capture. In desperation, Wickenburg began to hurl stones at the contrary beast--a further exercise in frustration, as the stones seemed to be too heavy to reach their mark. Upon examining the stones, Wickenburg found that their weight was due to the gold they contained, and thereby was discovered the Vulture Mine, one of the greatest gold discoveries in Arizona.

Those who work in the mines have another favorite animal, the mine rat. Rats are believed to give warning of impending cave-ins and bad gas, because they can sense the slightest movement in the surrounding rock and will scamper to safety when they do. It is considered bad luck to kill a mine rat. Rather, these underground creatures are carefully nurtured. They appear like clockwork at lunch hour and make a fine living from scraps tossed to them from miners' lunch pails. Old-timers who work in the mines often get to know the mine rats by name.

Although most prospecting stories concern the sudden wealth of those who make lucky discoveries, one story is told about an escaped convict named John Wilson who left his wealth to others. In 1880, while making his escape from Texas, Wilson visited two friends who were prospecting on Baxter Mountain in what is now New Mexico. After his arrival, Wilson climbed the mountain to take a look at the country beyond, carrying a pick with him. Halfway to the summit, he stopped to rest and began idly to chip pieces from the rock where he sat. The pieces appeared to be speckled with yellow. When he returned to the cabin, he turned over the chips to his friends, who let out a whoop. Even though it was now after dark, the three men climbed back to the spot by lantern light to mark it. The prospectors offered Wilson his share, but he said he had no use for gold and left the next day with nine silver dollars and a pistol given to him by his friends. The North and South Homestake claims, which Wilson had found, were later sold for $600,000, and the original strike has produced $3 million in ore.

There are many stories of lost mines, but none so tantalizing as that of the Lost Dutchman Mine in the Superstition Mountains east of Phoenix. The story begins with a young Mexican seeking refuge in the mountains from his sweetheart's angry father. Finding a gold deposit, he returned home and organized an expedition to carry out as much gold as possible before the land was turned over to the United States as part of the Gadsden Purchase. The Mexican party, laden with gold, set out for home but was ambushed by Apaches, who killed everyone except for two small boys who hid under a bush. The children eventually found their way home and, when they grew up, took a third partner and headed back to the mountains to locate the mine. As they were digging, a prospector with a long white beard named Jacob Wolz, known as the Dutchman, came upon them. Wolz had been driven into this part of the mountains by a band of Apaches. The Mexican boys told him the story of the mine, and later, as they slept, he killed them. Wolz made a number of trips out from the mine and back into the mountains, carrying gold ore to Phoenix. Stories of his strike spread, and many prospectors tried to trail him into the mountains. It is said that Wolz killed at least eight men who tried to find the mine. When he died in Phoenix about 1884, a shoebox full of gold ore was found under his bed. As he was dying, he told a friendly neighbor how to reach the mine. A key landmark in Wolz's directions, a tree with a peculiar-looking branch, could never be located, and the mine was never found. Literally thousands of amateur and professional prospectors have gone out in search of the Lost Dutchman Mine without success, and many have never returned.

Undoubtedly the most gruesome story about prospecting in the Southwest is a true one concerning a group of six prospectors who in 1873 headed out from Utah into the San Juan Mountains. They were part of a larger party which had gone as far as the Ute encampment, where the majority had decided to stay until spring because of the mountain snows. The six had pushed on, however, disregarding warnings of trouble ahead. Six weeks later, a lone member of the party, a man named Alfred Packer, reappeared out of the mountains with a tale of woe. He had been abandoned by his companions, he said, and forced to live on roots and small animals. Suspicions arose, however, when his first request was for whiskey, rather than food; and when he produced a considerable sum of money, after having claimed to be without funds, dark thoughts began to cross the minds of the others. Meanwhile, an Indian had come to the Indian agency where Packer had first appeared, carrying strips of flesh picked up along Packer's trail, which turned out to be human flesh. In the spring, a photographer for *Harper's Weekly* discovered the remains of five men whose skulls had been crushed and from whose bodies strips of flesh had been removed. Packer was arrested and charged with murder. He claimed that starvation had driven his companions mad and that he had killed one of them in self-defense, then discovered that the one he had killed had apparently slain the other four. There was no jail handy, and Packer was chained to a rock but made his escape. He was recaptured in Wyoming ten years later, tried for murder, and sentenced to be hanged by the neck until dead. His conviction was overturned on a technicality. He was retried, found guilty of manslaughter, and sentenced to forty years. A few years later he was paroled and died in Denver in 1906.

Precious metals were not the only sources of quick fortune in the Southwest. After the gold and silver fever had begun to subside, new quests replaced it. In central Arizona an army scout found copper near Jerome and staked out a claim. Dr. James Douglas, an expert employed by Phelps Dodge & Company, inspected the claim and decided that it was not worth bothering with. Shortly thereafter William A. Clark, who had built a successful copper mining enterprise at Butte, Montana, took a look at the claim and bought it immediately. By the time it had played out, the copper mine at Jerome produced $60 million. Dr. Douglas did not let down his employers, however. He wandered farther south to a small town called Bisbee, where he bought a claim for Phelps Dodge which came to be known as the Copper Queen. It produced two billion pounds of copper at a net profit of $100 million.

Still another source of fortune was tapped from the earth when Anthony F. Lucas teamed up with Pattillo Higgins to drill exploratory oil wells in Texas. Lucas was an engineer with experience in mining sulphur; Higgins was a wildcat oil driller who was down on his luck. Together they drilled a well into a salt mound in east Texas, and on January 11, 1902, the famous Spindletop oil well blew in with a geyser of black gold rising almost 200 feet into the air, signaling the beginning of the age of oil in the West. Unlike gold and silver prospecting, which could be carried on by prospectors operating on a shoestring, hunting for oil was an expensive gamble which required financial investment in equipment and labor. But the West did not want for men who were willing to put up the capital. Even though nine out of ten efforts produced only dry holes, the number of successful drillings more than compensated.

In the middle of the twentieth century, a new prospecting boom began with the development of nuclear fission and the need for large stocks of uranium. An electrical contractor in Minneapolis whose shop had caught fire, forcing him to move out, purchased a trailer and headed for a new life in Mexico. Along the way he began to hear stories of uranium finds and decided to try his luck. He purchased some books and a Geiger counter and headed into the Colorado Plateau. After several months of searching he turned up an ore bed in the wastelands of Utah which earned him $10 million. His name was Vernon Pick.

Another twentieth-century uranium prospector, Charlie Steen, was fired up from reading an article in a mining journal and spent two and a half years wandering back and forth across Utah. Operating on a shoestring and often desperate for funds, Steen pressed on. Then one day, with a borrowed drill, he obtained some samples of ore, took them into Moab for appraisal, and discovered that he had found one of the richest uranium beds in the West, converting him into a millionaire overnight. Unfortunately, Steen's story does not end there. His was a career of rags to riches and back to rags again because of excessive spending and unwise investments. The folk around Moab say that Charlie Steen still wanders the countryside in hopes of repeating his first miraculous discovery.

The uranium prospecting fever spread, and throughout the Southwest fortune seekers riding in jeeps and armed with Geiger counters bounced across canyons and deserts hunting for their pots of gold. Some found them. Even today, as you visit Canyonlands and Arches national parks, and Dead Horse Point State Park, you can hear tales of the great discoveries made by hardy fortune seekers who traversed that same country only a few years ago.

THE OUTLAWS

The Southwest produced not only fortunes but also many remarkable men. One of the most remarkable was Robert LeRoy Parker, son of Mormon parents, who was born and raised in the small town of Circleville, Utah. He became the renowned Butch Cassidy, the good-natured leader of a gang of outlaws called the Wild Bunch, which preyed on the West for almost thirty years. A sort of Robin Hood, Butch Cassidy is said never to have killed a man and never to have turned down a request for help.

The Wild Bunch was a loose organization made up of several smaller groups, including Kid Curry's gang, Bob Lee's rustlers, Black Jack Ketchum's train robbers, and a smattering of others. Sometimes they acted separately, but at other times they worked together under Butch Cassidy's leadership, constituting one of the largest outlaw bands in the history of the West. Cassidy and Kid Curry perfected the science of train robbery to the point of carrying dynamite to blow up any express-car strong room which carried gold and securities. Although their prinicipal headquarters was Hole in the Wall in Star Valley, along the border between Wyoming and Utah, they also used other hideouts throughout the Southwest. Butch is reported to have used Capitol Gorge on occasion as an escape route. Unlike Cassidy, Kid Curry was a killer, who frequently shot for the fun of it. Curry was the original advocate of train robberies, staging a few successful robberies on his own and showing how lucrative they could be. The gangs worked together to plague the Union Pacific and

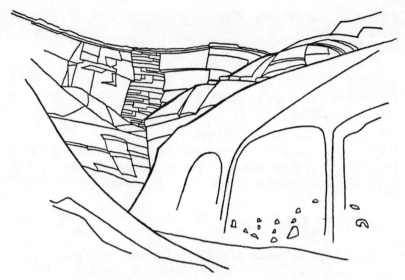

Capitol Gorge (Capitol Reef National Park)

Great Northern railroads. The railroads countered by hiring the Pinkerton organization, which committed extensive manpower to efforts at tracking down the outlaws.

Along the trail of robberies was a trail of bloodshed. Kid Curry killed Sheriff Joseph Hazen following a robbery of the Union Pacific at Wilcox, Wyoming. Following Hazen's death, Sheriff John Hyler and his deputy Sam Jenkins, of Grand County, Utah, flushed one of the gang from a hideout and killed him in the ensuing gun fight. When Kid Curry heard of the killing, he rode to Moab, Utah, called Hyler and Jenkins out into the street, and killed them both. He stepped over the bodies, mounted his horse, and rode out of town. Posses followed him without success. Other lawmen bit the dust at Curry's hands. In between raids, Curry would sometimes go back home to Missouri to visit his mother, who had no idea of his activities.

Butch Cassidy tried to restrain Kid Curry's violence. Cassidy upbraided Curry for shooting down an Adams Express Company guard in one holdup. On another occasion, as the Wild Bunch was robbing a train in Montana, Kid Curry pointed a gun at the conductor (who had twice before been on trains held up by the gang) when the conductor disregarded an order to stop as he went to set the brakes on the last car of the train. Cassidy knocked Curry's gun away, saying quietly, "Let him alone, Kid."

But Cassidy was not always around to caution restraint. When Kid Curry learned that a cattleman named Winters had reported some of his activities to the authorities, he and his brothers rode 400 miles to take vengeance on Winters. Winters, forewarned, killed one of the brothers. Kid Curry waited patiently until one day he saw Winters, called his name, and shot him as he went for his gun. He rode over to the spot where Winters fell and emptied his revolver into the dying man.

In San Antonio, a cowboy got into an argument with a member of Curry's gang who was deaf. The cowboy challenged the deaf man to draw, but Curry pushed his fellow gang member to one side and took his place, outdrawing the cowboy and killing him. The rest of the cowboy's outfit came on the run. Curry put his pistol back in its holster. "Anybody want to slap leather, let's go," he said. No one did. He mounted up and quietly rode out of town. The rewards for his capture rose to $40,000.

Finally, as the West became more developed, Butch Cassidy met with Kid Curry and told him that he was moving out to South America. He asked Curry to come along, but the Kid refused. The two men agreed to make one last strike together. They held up the Great Northern on August 24, 1901, taking $41,500. Then the gang rode to Fort Worth, Texas, where they posed for a formal photograph in derbies and dark suits which has become one of the great items of Wild Western Americana. After a riotous few days of champagne, rich food, and parties at Fanny Porter's Sporting House, Cassidy and Harry Longbaugh ("The Sundance Kid"), together with Etta Place, a pretty young schoolteacher, left for New York and then South America.

Kid Curry kept roaming his old haunts, evading the Pinkertons and the Union Pacific detectives. Finally he was arrested in Knoxville, Tennessee, after shooting down two police officers and spraining a leg while trying to escape. After a two-week trial, he was sentenced to life imprisonment, but the day before he was to be sent to the Federal prison in Columbus, Ohio, he escaped, using a noose made out of broom wire to lasso the keeper and taking his keys. Stealing the sheriff's horse, he rode out of town at a leisurely pace, precipitating one of the biggest manhunts in the history of the country. In June of 1903, following a train robbery, a gang was trapped in a canyon near Glendale Springs, Colorado. One of the gang volunteered to hold off the posse while the rest escaped. At dawn, a shot rang out, and the posse entered to find Tap Duncan, alias Kid Curry, with a bullet put through his head by his own pistol.

Meanwhile, Butch Cassidy and his companions had gone on a rampage through Peru, Bolivia, and Chile, holding up trains and banks in true Western style. Finally the Bolivian army was called out to stop them. They were cornered and all killed in a final desperate gun battle. (Some say Etta escaped the fate of the men, but no one knows for sure.)

The Wild Bunch did not lay sole claim to being the only colorful outlaws of the Southwest. One bandit who gained a reputation on his own was William H. Bonney, born in New York City and raised in Kansas and New Mexico, who committed his first murder at the age of twelve by stabbing a man who had insulted his mother. Earning the nickname Billy the Kid, the bloodthirsty young man rode a trail that scattered blood throughout the Southwest. He killed three Indians in Arizona for their blankets and ponies, then killed a soldier at Fort Bowie. After fleeing to Mexico, he killed at least three more men and engaged in some horse stealing. By the time he had reached the age of seventeen, he had returned to Texas, where he killed eight Indians in order to save a wagon train. Then he teamed up with Jesse Evans and started stealing horses and selling them across the Rio Grande, committing three more murders along the way. During the cattle-rustling war in Lincoln County, New Mexico, Billy the Kid became outraged when a wealthy Englishman who had financed one of the herds, and who was arrested while he was battling with some rustlers, was murdered by members of a deputy sheriff's posse after he had surrendered and turned over his gun. Billy killed Sheriff Brady in retaliation. Finally, at the age of twenty-two, Billy the Kid was captured by Sheriff Pat Garrett and sentenced to be hanged. Because he had unusually small hands and large wrists, he managed to shake off his handcuffs by going without food for several days. He killed his guard and the jailer, did a jig on the jail balcony, then made his escape on horseback, still wearing a leg iron. A year later Sheriff Garrett tracked him down in Fort Sumner, where he was killed in the gunfire while trying to avoid capture.

Black Jack Ketchum, another Southwestern train-robbing specialist who occasionally joined the Wild Bunch, came into Arizona from Texas. He had managed to escape several posses, until he singlehandedly held up a train at Twin-Mountain Curve. He was wounded in making his escape and was found wandering in the desert the following morning. At his hanging, the nervous hangman fumbled with the noose, and Black Jack is quoted as having said, "Hurry it up, hurry it up. I'm due in hell for dinner."

Among the lesser outlaws of the Southwest who were not without their touch of color was Clay Allison of Colfax County, New Mexico. Allison got into an argument with another desperado, named Chunk. Chunk invited Allison to dinner at the local hotel, and each man ate with his pistol on the table. When coffee was served, they each used their guns to stir the brew. Chunk, after stirring his coffee, instead of laying his pistol back on the table, proceeded to slip it under the table. He fired at Allison and missed. Allison then fired point blank, and Chunk fell forward on his plate.

Another outlaw, a rustler named Joe Asque, hid out on Carrizo Flats to escape a sheriff's posse. Seeing a number of horses there, he could not resist the temptation to string up five of the best saddle horses and start east. Suddenly two men in a wagon approached and pointed a rifle at him. They took his gun and saddle, stood him in their wagon, tied his hands with his own rope, put another length over the branch of a nearby tree, and tied it around his neck. Then they moved their wagon away and left Asque dangling. Because of his light weight, and the fact that the knot in the rope was under his chin, he managed to survive long enough to free his hands and cut the rope with his pocket knife. As he told about the experience later, he said the hanging was not so bad, but it made him angry to have to ride his horse bareback for a hundred miles to get back home.

THE COWBOYS

Cattle raising moved westward with the frontier. By 1865 the principal areas supplying cattle for eastern markets were in Illinois and Iowa. Then, in 1866, the first longhorn cattle from Texas crossed the Red River into Indian territory and were moved up into Missouri and Kansas with hopes on the part of their owners of sales to packers in Iowa and Illinois. The skinny creatures with their wide horns provided a good return for their hides, but the beef was tough and gamey and hard to sell. Then new waves of immigrants from Eastern Europe, with a tradition of home-style sausages, began buying the cheap Western beef, spicing it heavily, and making tasty meat products. The prosperity of the Southwest from cattle grazing began to grow. As the years went by, every acre of pasture land was put to use in fattening animals for market, and new strains of cattle were soon introduced to raise the quality of the meat.

The men who made this industry flourish were the cowboys. They rode hard in the saddle from morning till night, through summer heat and winter cold, with few holidays and not much pay. The principal diversion of these tough outdoorsmen was sitting around the evening campfire swapping stories and smoking. Card playing was frowned on because it encouraged late hours and sometimes led to quarrels.

Most of the cowboys in the Southwest came from Texas, and their equipment and clothing are essentially Texan in character. One of the unique by-products of cowboy existence is today's Western saddle. It is an evolution of the Spanish-Mexican saddle of California, originally an elaborate and cumbersome object, heavily decorated in gold or silver. Today, the making of a Western saddle is still regarded as an art. The wooden frame is made of Oregon pine, prized for its lightness, elasticity, and strength. It is carefully shaped to fit both horse and rider. The various structural parts of the saddle are attached by mortising, and the whole is then covered with wet rawhide which is allowed to shrink in place. Next come the various leather pieces needed to cover the pommel, seat, and cantle, and finally the stirrup straps and fenders. The Western saddle is the prize possession of its owner and is guarded carefully. A story is told of a schoolboy out West whose teacher asked him who Benedict Arnold was. The boy answered, "He was a man who sold his saddle."

The cowboys were a rough crowd. A drunken cowboy shot and wounded an Indian on the street in Farmington, New Mexico, one day in 1883, and several hundred Indians threatened to go back on the warpath. A few years later, Farmington's first resident preacher got into the bad graces of a bunch of local cowboys when he refused to drink with them. Several of them showed their displeasure by shooting holes in the floor around his feet. The preacher stood his ground. A traveling stereopticon operator, who set up a canvas screen and put on a show in Farmington, did not have such steely nerves. When the cowboys started to shoot holes in his canvas screen, the showman jumped out the window.

The cattle business had its ups and downs in the Southwest and was finally supplanted by cultivation of the land in those parts of the country which proved to be unsuitable for raising cattle.

Horses and mules were not the only animals used to carry the burdens of man across the Southwest. There was a brief ill-fated attempt to introduce camels as an experiment in desert transportation. Edward Fitzgerald Beale was one of the officers sent to meet General Kearny and escort him on his march across the Southwest during the Mexican War. Beale was a man of enthusiasm who had joined the Navy when he was fourteen. On the march with Kearny, he had the inspiration that camels would make good beasts of burden in the desert climate. His opportunity came when he was sent to Washington with Kit Carson to report on the Kearny expedition. There he sold Jefferson Davis, then Secretary of War, on the idea. Secretary

Davis sent representatives to North Africa and Turkey to purchase thirty-three camels and hire several drivers. The camels
landed in Texas in 1856. The following year, forty-seven more
were imported, and all were used to open a route through an
unexplored wilderness from Fort Defiance across Arizona to the
Colorado River. The camels proved remarkably adaptable to the
climate, traveling between 25 and 30 miles a day and carrying
water for the mules accompanying the wagon train, in addition
to their own burden of 600 pounds of supplies. They climbed
through snow-covered mountains, forded streams, and crossed
the desert with ease. They had only one major drawback—they
caused stampedes among the cattle, horses, and mules, who were
frightened at their strange appearance. Moreover, it was impossible to find drivers for them, and only one of the original Arab
camel drivers stuck it out. Finally, the Civil War cut short the
experiment. Many of the camels were sold. Others escaped and
wandered off into the desert. The single Arab driver, lured by
tales of fortune, became a prospector. Stories were told throughout the Southwest of the camels being encountered on moonlit
nights, moving quietly as ghosts and frightening domestic animals. Mule skinners shot them on sight; others hunted them.
Some were caught and used to carry ore. One recurring legend
concerned a great beast who was seen carrying a dead rider
strapped to his back. As the legend evolved, the rider slowly
disintegrated, until finally only a pair of legs remained. When
the animal was finally shot, only the rawhide straps which had
served to tie the rider on were still attached to the beast.

During this time when the population was growing rapidly
and the range land of the cattle was expanding across country,
firearms became an important part of the Western scene. Originally there were a number of makers whose products were used
on the frontier, but Samuel Colt, who had ambitions for his
shiny new factory in Hartford, Connecticut, decided upon a
competitive public relations program, writing to his agent in
Arizona, James Dean Alden, and complaining that the news-
papers were publishing complimentary notices about other makes
of guns "and their use upon Grisly Bears, Indians, Mexicans,

&c &c. Now this is all wrong—it should be published Colt's Rifles, Carbines, &c." Colt went on to advise his man to present the editor with a pistol or a rifle if it would do any good, adding, "You know how to do this, & Do not forget to have his Columns report all the accidents that occur to the Sharps & other humbug arms." Before long the Colt had become the cowboys' favorite weapon.

The most lasting contribution the cowboys made to the West was their collection of tall stories which have been absorbed into the lore of the country. They told a story about one of their fellows who had a habit of sleeping when the rest of the crew was working. His colleagues decided to teach him a lesson. One day when they found him curled up in a haystack sound asleep, they killed a tarantula and placed it close to him. Then they pricked him in the leg a couple of times with a pin. Having awakened him, one of the crew rushed up immediately and smashed the tarantula. The erstwhile sleeper, still groggy, was filled with fright upon seeing the dead tarantula and began to have symptoms of illness as his colleagues recounted terrible stories of the painful deaths they had seen come from tarantula bites. Then one of the gang offered to try a remedy he had heard once in an effort to save the cowboy. First a pint of bear's oil was put down the cowboy's throat, followed by a glass of soda, a cup of vinegar, and finally a quart of water in which a plug of tobacco had been permitted to soak. The cowboy was cured, not only of his tarantula bite but also of his habit of sleeping on the job.

They told another story about old man Yost, who decided to make a fortune from a herd of turtles. Yost, having lost his savings in the cattle business, learned that turtles brought a price up North for making turtle soup. Figuring that terrapins would bring about two dollars a head, he sent his cowboys out with gunnysacks to collect all they could find. Before long he had 14,986 terrapins. Then they headed north, driving the terrapins. The first day they made a quarter of a mile, and Yost figured out that it would take 5,600 days to reach market. But when he thought of the profits he decided to go on. Months later the herd finally reached Red River. But his former partner, from whom he had parted on bad terms, having learned of Yost's herd, had reached the river ahead of him, and as Yost pushed the turtles into the river, he saw someone in a boat place an object on a log in the middle of the stream. When the turtle herd reached the log, every last one of them suddenly dove to the bottom of the river and drowned. Yost's former partner had put a diving mud turtle in front of his dry-terrapin herd. Yost figured that he had lost somewhere around half a million dollars. So the story goes.

One of the devices used in rustling cattle was to change the brand slightly to assert new ownership. There is a story concerning a rancher whose brand was "IC." A rustler changed the brand to read "ICU." The rancher then reclaimed his cattle by rebranding them "ICU2."

Another short story about Western gunplay concerns the cowboy who came up to his friend and said, "Didn't you tell me that Tex Parker called me a hotheaded, obnoxious s.o.b.?"

"Naw, I never said that."

"Doggone! I've gone and killed an innocent man."

Practical jokes are also part of cowboy lore. A favorite prank on new arrivals from the East was the "badger fight." An air of mystery would be created about something that was going to happen on a particular evening, calculated to stir the curiosity of the new arrival. After allowing themselves to be pressed by the newcomer, the cowboys would tell him that there was going to be a badger fight. "Ever see one?" The newcomer would then be told in confidence that he would be taken to see the fight if he promised not to tell anybody about it. That night, the tenderfoot would be led to a nearby stable, where there would be a wooden box in the middle of the floor, supposedly containing a half-starved badger. Somebody would have brought along a fierce-looking dog. The newcomer would be given the privilege of pulling the rope to upset the box. As he yanked on the rope, out would come a white chamber pot. The tenderfoot would then be given the opportunity to buy drinks all around.

Among the tallest of the tall stories, embellished with each retelling, were those relating to the weather, whose extremes, ranging from intense heat in summer to bitter cold in winter, were a regular part of the cowboys' occupational hazards. They slept many nights out on the open range on a "Tucson bed"—the ground underneath, lying on their stomachs with their backs for a cover—and they had to learn to get along with the weather. If newcomers were not hardy to begin with, they surely became so after a short time on the job. Theirs was truly an outdoor life and they were quickly toughened up. The story of the cowboy who went for a swim, told in Chapter 1, sums up pretty well the changeable nature of the weather which even a visitor on a summer holiday is likely to encounter in the Southwest. From the heat of Utah, it is only a few hours' drive to the occasional summertime snow and hail one may find in Colorado.

As for the winter weather, one cowboy claimed that it got so cold at the ranch where he worked one winter that when the foreman came out to give orders the words froze as they came out of his mouth and the men had to break them off one by one so they could tell what he was saying.

On another occasion, it seems that two green hands who were sent out one cold winter day to put up some fence poles found the ground covered with frozen rattlesnakes. Deciding to save some money, they drove the snakes into the ground instead of cutting poles. The next day they were fired. The snakes had thawed out and crawled off with several miles of good barbed wire.

The Southwestern climate can be changeable in the winter as well as in the summer. It is said that there was once a cowboy who, after he lit his candle one cold winter evening, saw that the candle flame had frozen. He had to wait until it thawed before he could blow his candle out. When the sun came up in the morning, it grew so warm that the corn he had for his cattle began to pop. His horse thought the popcorn was snow and almost froze to death.

THE RAILROADS

The California Gold Rush of 1849, when thousands crossed

the continent on foot, horseback, mule, or behind oxen, raised a hue and cry for the construction of a railroad across the plains to the Pacific. Topographical engineers were sent out into the field to survey a route, and many officials in Washington argued the necessity of building a railroad for military purposes as well as commercial benefits. Disagreement over whether the route should be a northern one or a southern one delayed construction until the outbreak of the Civil War. In July, 1862, Congress passed the Pacific Railroad Act, authorizing a route along the forty-second parallel. Under the terms of the act, the builders of the railroad were offered a right of way through public domain, with cash subsidies of $16,000 a mile on the plains and from $32,000 to $48,000 a mile through the mountains. The act also offered a bounty of sections of public land in a checkerboard pattern for 20 miles on each side of the tracks, as well as free use of building materials from the public lands. Two railroad companies, the Union Pacific in the East and the Central Pacific in the West, were organized to do the job, working from the two ends to meet in the middle. The work progressed slowly, and rails did not really begin to move until 1866. Parties of engineers, keeping one eye peeled for Indians, went on ahead to mark the route, followed up by husky gangs of construction workers. Logistical problems of supplying the operation were staggering. To lay one mile of track required about forty cars to move up rails, railroad supplies, and other necessities. The Union Pacific was saved from financial disaster in 1867 by reaching Cheyenne, Wyoming, beyond which the bounty jumped from $16,000 to $48,000 a mile. The two companies began to race in breakneck competition for the financial prizes that were provided by Congress. The proposed junction point kept moving as the progress developed. In time, amid some confusion and lack of official decisiveness, the two railroad lines, instead of joining, overlapped, often running close together, and the competing crews of workmen—Irishmen on the Union Pacific and Chinese on the Central Pacific—engaged in fierce rivalry. The violence reached a point where the Irishmen blasted their dynamite without warning the Chinese, blowing many of them to kingdom come. The Chinese quietly reciprocated, blasting a number of Irishmen to their reward. Finally, in 1869, Congress designated Promontory, Utah, as the point of junction. After many comic-opera delays, a formal ceremony took place there on May 10, 1869, as a golden spike was struck by a silver hammer where the two railroads came together. California's governor, Leland Stanford, was accorded the honor of striking the first blow. The hammer and the spike were each connected to a telegraph line so that, as they made contact, the signal would be transmitted to cities across the country. Governor Stanford missed. The telegraph operator, thinking quickly, simulated the blow with his telegraph key, and nationwide celebrations were unleashed as the telegraph operator flashed the news that "the Pacific Railroad is finished."

Other branch railroads were built throughout the Southwest, some marked by strenuous competition. Between 1876 and 1879 a bitter struggle raged between the Denver & Rio Grande Railroad and the Atchison, Topeka & Santa Fe, which flared up on several occasions. The Denver & Rio Grande had built its line as far west as Cañon City, Colorado, but did not appear to be interested in moving farther on. Local residents then organized the Cañon City & San Juan Railroad and filed surveys with the Secretary of the Interior. The Santa Fe Railroad, taking an interest in the possibilities, sent a crew of workers by mule team from Pueblo to the mouth of the Royal Gorge Canyon, a deep narrow cleft which had been declared impassable. Meanwhile the Denver & Rio Grande Railroad dispatched a crew from Cañon City. The Denver & Rio Grande crew arrived at the canyon just thirty minutes before the Santa Fe men and had started grading a right of way when the competition appeared. Each crew would lay rails by day and tear up the competition's rails by night. Guns were much in evidence, but no one was killed. Finally the dispute was transferred to the courts. A similar race to lay tracks through Raton Pass, where Uncle Dick Wootton had successfully operated his private toll road, took place sometime later. In February, 1878, the Denver & Rio Grande sent a construction crew to the pass from Pueblo. A few hours later, the Santa Fe sent its construction crew by special train. Arriving at eleven o'clock at night, the Santa Fe men were sent immediately into the mountains. When the Rio Grande crew set out for work the following morning, they found the Santa Fe men already grading the track bed. In the end the dispute was resolved by the Rio Grande abandoning any claim to the Raton Pass route and the Santa Fe agreeing not to contest the route through the Royal Gorge.

One of the ways the railroad companies increased their profits was by constructing towns along their rights of way. Durango, Colorado, was one such town, founded in 1880 by the Denver & Rio Grande Railroad. During its early period, Durango was a roughshod community. The cattle industry had a large share in its growth. Cowboys, prospectors, miners, gamblers, freight men, and railroad construction crews all mingled, frequently engaging in fights. Law and order was maintained by vigilantes. Mail was brought in by persons who happened to go that way and was dumped in a cracker box in a corner of the general store. Court was held in a large room over the store. Water, hauled for some distance, sold for forty cents a barrel. An attempt to operate a streetcar line was abandoned because of the crews' abusive conduct and their habit of pulling the cars out of the station before all the passengers could get aboard. A pioneer editor, Dave Day, started publishing the Durango *Herald-Democrat* in 1892 and was so direct and profane in his comments that he was frequently sued for libel. There is a story about Day's attendance at a Denver political rally. One of the speakers at the rally was Congressman Jim Belford. The congressman spoke at some length, and after a while Day stretched himself out full length across the chairs directly below the speaker's platform. The congressman announced that he would soon conclude his remarks, to which Day is said to have replied, "Don't hurry, Jim. We can lie down here as long as you can lie up there."

6
The Modern Indian

During World War II, the Japanese proved to be extremely adept at breaking military codes. Whenever American troops used radios and walkie-talkies to relay battle orders, the Japanese were usually able to intercept the American advances because of the ease with which they deciphered orders given in code. The Americans became desperate. They resorted to pig-Latin, but even this was pierced by the enemy. Then someone had a brainstorm. Communications teams chosen from the 3,500 Navajo Indians serving in the armed forces were assigned to man battle-field radios. The Navajos relayed orders in their native tongue, which only a few outsiders knew. The Japanese were thrown into confusion and the American forces were able to move forward, protected by the use of a strange language which tribal tradition had kept alive for hundreds of years—probably the only tongue Japanese intelligence had not been able to master. The experience served to remind top military officers that the Indians of the Southwest still maintained a staunch independence.

There is a story told in the West about an Indian who applied for a bank loan. The bank officer asked the Indian what he could put up as collateral. The Indian replied, "Me gottum five hundred horses." The banker approved the loan with the horses as security. In due course the Indian returned to the bank with a large roll of bills and paid off the loan. The banker, seeing that the Indian still had a substantial amount of cash left, suggested that he might want to deposit the money in the bank. The Indian looked at the bank officer suspiciously and asked, "How many horses you gottum?"

This story is more than a silly joke. It illustrates graphically the basic difference in philosophy and outlook between white men and Indians. That difference has been at the heart of the bitterness in relations between the two races almost from the first moment white men set foot on American soil. The difference has been reflected in dealings over land, hunting rights, possessions, and, ultimately, peace and war. The difference still exists today, and the only way for a visitor to understand and appreciate the Indians of the Southwest is to make an effort to see things from the Indian point of view.

Historically, the difference in philosophy between Indians and white men can be summed up in the phrase "Indian giver." This epithet exemplifies the fact that the Indians originally had no concept of private property rights. One of the basic cultural differences noted by the Spaniards when they arrived in the Southwest, and still true today, was the fact that the Indians thought of the land as belonging to all people, to be used and enjoyed by everyone. When the colonists "purchased" land from the Indians, they thought they were acquiring absolute title according to European standards of private property. The Indians, on the other hand, believed that they were merely agreeing to share the land with the white men. When the Indians returned to hunt on the land, misunderstandings were bound to follow. Indian and white man alike thought each had been cheated by the other. The same conceptual difference frequently applied to personal property. In the beginning the Indians gladly shared their meager food supplies with white colonists as an expression of hospitality, but when the colonists prospered and the Indians sought the same hospitality in return they were driven off as thieves.

This difference in viewpoint has led to bitter experiences even in modern times. After the Indians were assigned to reservations, a white reform movement attempted to force on the Indians the ownership of individual lots as a way to teach frugality and responsibility. All that it taught them was the pain and frustration that came from being cheated by speculators who bought their land for under its true value and then turned them out.

When one stops to think about it, there is a special kind of beauty to the notion that all of the earth belongs to everyone and that men share what they have with those in need. It can even be related to certain other religious teachings if one is so minded. It is part of this philosophy that leads to the Indians' respect for nature and their belief that each plant and animal has a soul of its own. White men have only recently discovered the meaning of ecology and conservation. Indians have been living it for generations.

As a visitor it is difficult, if not impossible, truly to see within the Indian life style and feel a sense of participation, but with sympathy and good will it is possible to learn something of what made the Indians the way they were and the way they are today. In fact, one of the greatest pleasures to be derived from a trip to the Southwest is the glimpse it provides of the life and outlook of the Indians who live there. One comes away with a broadened view of man and his environment.

There are five major groups of Indians in the Colorado Plateau section of the Southwest which can be visited and learned about to some extent: the Navajos, the Hopis, the Rio Grande Pueblo Indians, the Zuñis, and the Utes. Some have shown a better ability than others to survive the ravages of defeat and time spent in an alien culture. This ability is visible today, ranging from the vitality and determination to succeed of the Navajos to the near destruction of the once-proud Utes. A close-up view of these people on their home ground not only provides information of great interest but also a philosophical perspective. Attitude is everything—if one approaches the Indian of the Southwest with a superior or snickering outlook, one will see only a superficial tourist's picture, but if one approaches with respect for the Indian's own identity and with the good taste not to intrude on his privacy, one will see a broad and fascinating picture from which can be gained much that is profound and lasting.

THE NAVAJOS

In trying to understand the Indians of the Southwest, the best place to begin is with the Navajos. They are the most populous, the most successful in adapting to their environment, and they have managed to maintain their integrity despite modern developments in their economy and government.

In 1864 hundreds of Navajo Indians set out on a forced march which makes the infamous Bataan "Death March" of 1942 seem like a Sunday outing. On March 6, 1864, following a devastating military operation led by Colonel Kit Carson, 2,400 persons, 400 horses, 3,000 sheep and goats, and 30 wagons carrying children and cripples began the "Long Walk"—300 miles from Fort Defiance to Fort Sumner, southeast of Santa Fe. Additional marches were conducted over the ensuing months, until eventually 8,000 Navajos were placed in captivity at Fort Sumner. The Long Walk was the climax of a series of raids which Colonel Carson had made against the Navajos, who had themselves been regularly raiding the colonists' Rio Grande settlements while the army was preoccupied with the Civil War. Carson, whose orders were to put a stop to this raiding by the Navajos, had followed a scorched-earth policy in rounding them up. He had killed their crops in order to force them into submission. Starvation finally took its toll, and the Navajos straggled into Fort Defiance to surrender. Once the majority of them had given in, they were forced to march the 300 miles across the hot desert. The idea behind the march was to remove them from their stronghold in Canyon de Chelly and to pacify them by teaching them to farm. The effort was a dismal failure. The land they were placed on at Bosque Redondo was poor, and the small amount of available water was bitter. Illness swept through the camp, causing hundreds to die of dysentery and pneumonia. The result was a major calamity. The illness, the hunger, the homesickness, and the destruction of their pride were a profoundly embittering experience for the Navajo people.

The experimental relocation at Bosque Redondo reached a state of total collapse after insects, drought, floods, and raids by other Indians reduced the Navajos to abjectivity. Finally, in the spring of 1868, they refused to plant any more crops. A commission was sent out from Washington to negotiate the Navajos' return to their homeland, and a reservation was set aside with Canyon de Chelly at its heart. The size of the Navajo reservation has expanded over the years until now it occupies more than 15 million acres. The Navajo population has also expanded, literally almost exploding—from approximately 7,000 in 1868 to over 100,000 today. Although many Navajos live and work today in modern white man's structures, a substantial number still follow traditional patterns of life, religion, and livelihood.

Navajo dress has been borrowed almost entirely from the white man. Navajo men and boys wear variations of the standard cowboy costume: blue denim pants, bright shirts and scarves, and large felt hats. The women wear long, full skirts and bright velveteen blouses, largely patterned after the clothing worn in the 1860's by the wives of the army officers at Fort Sumner. Those ladies bestowed some old gowns upon the Indian women, and the full skirts of the present day evolved from these hand-me-downs, worn by the Navajo women without their original hoops. Despite these borrowings from the white man, Navajo Indian men still wear breechcloths under their trousers, and the women adorn themselves with distinctive handmade Navajo jewelry.

Tradition-conscious Navajos live in their own style of dwelling, called a "hogan." Usually constructed of stone or logs and mud, this structure is generally six-sided, with a front opening facing east and a smoke hole at the center of the top. In summertime it is customary to provide a cooler place to sleep, while tending crops or a flock of sheep, by building a shelter out of brush, often removed some distance from the winter hogan. The Navajo residential compound often includes additional structures for animals, and sometimes two or more hogans may be built

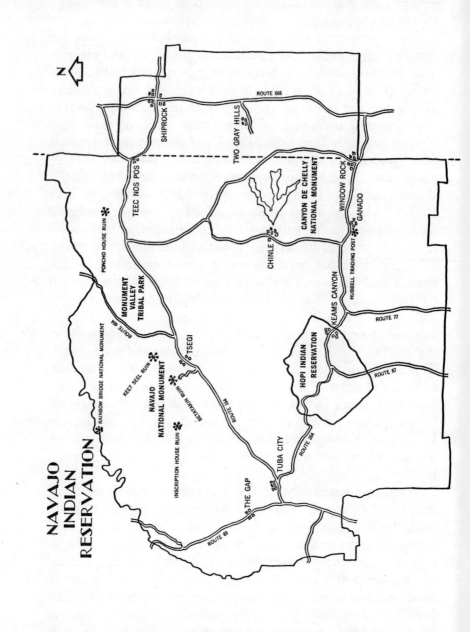

NAVAJO
INDIAN
RESERVATION

ROUTE 666

SHIPROCK

TWO GRAY HILLS

TEEC NOS POS

PONCHO HOUSE RUIN

CANYON DE CHELLY NATIONAL MONUMENT

CHINLE

WINDOW ROCK

GANADO

HUBBELL TRADING POST

RAINBOW BRIDGE NATIONAL MONUMENT

ROUTE 464

MONUMENT VALLEY TRIBAL PARK

KEET SEEL RUIN

NAVAJO NATIONAL MONUMENT

BETATAKIN RUIN

TSEGI

KEAMS CANYON

ROUTE 77

HOPI INDIAN RESERVATION

ROUTE 87

INSCRIPTION HOUSE RUIN

ROUTE 164

ROUTE 264

TUBA CITY

THE GAP

ROUTE 89

fairly close together to be occupied by relatives. The hogan is a one-room affair, usually about 25 feet in diameter, which serves all of the members of the family. The women sit on the south side, and the men on the north. The male head of the family and distinguished visitors sit on the west side, facing the doorway. Various household items are located around the room, including dried herbs, ceremonial equipment, hunting equipment, and articles of clothing. Trunks and suitcases are used to store extra clothing and bedding. The fire is in the center of the room, and pots and pans are stacked nearby. Cupboards for food supplies, usually made of boxes, are placed near the door. There are seldom any heavy pieces of furniture in the hogan, although frequently stoves and beds may be found, and occasionally a table.

The Navajo family usually keeps the same hours for both adults and children. The whole family retires at an early hour, sleeping on sheepskins and blankets which are spread on the floor at night and which, weather permitting, are hung out of doors for airing during the daytime. When it is necessary to have two sittings for a meal because of the size of the family, the men and boys eat first and the women later, although ordinarily the family eats together. It is not unusual for a family to share a common bowl, using spoons and bread as eating utensils.

The white man has had an impact on the eating habits of the Navajo family, which nowadays purchases most of its food from the trading post. The family's meat, however, is still often home-raised, usually consisting of mutton, goat, and beef. Their staple foods are bread and meat. They eat very few green vegetables, but this deficiency is more than made up for by their practice of eating the internal organs and all other edible portions of the animals they slaughter, which thereby provide them with needed vitamins and minerals. Indeed, the soundness of the Navajos' teeth and the infrequency of cavities suggest that their eating habits may be substantially better than the white man's. Eating tends to be feast or famine for the Navajos, who will live for many days on a diet consisting primarily of bread and coffee and then eat substantially for two or three days when an animal has been slaughtered.

Personal cleanliness varies from family to family. It is not unusual to find lice and other vermin in hogans and on the Indians who reside therein. Delousing, as with many other native peoples, tends to be a social activity. Daily washing of face and hands is customary, but bathing is not frequent. The reason is self-evident—water must frequently be hauled some distance.

The division of labor between men and women tends to follow the traditional pattern of the white man. The menfolk are generally responsible for building dwellings and fences and tending the fields and the livestock. The womenfolk do the butchering of animals and the cooking and look after the children. Any spare time they may have is spent weaving and occasionally making pots or baskets. Recreation includes hunting, foot racing, singing, and storytelling.

The Navajo Indians derive their principal income from raising sheep and goats and sometimes horses. They earn some supplementary income from the crops they grow and from jewelry making and weaving. Navajo blankets, one of the best-known native crafts, are usually woven of wool which comes from the family's own sheep.

Although they are an aggressive and hard-working people, the Navajos are also extremely kind, especially to their children and to their old people.

Their native religion continues to maintain a strong place in the lives of the Navajos. Its basic conceptual framework is the existence of two spiritual groups of people, the Earth Surface People (from whom the present Navajos are descended) and the Holy People. The Holy People are so designated not because of moral quality but because of their mystery and power. They travel on lightning, sunbeams, and rainbows, and they have the power either to help or to hurt the Earth Surface People. According to Navajo belief, the Holy People originally lived beneath the surface of the earth and were driven to the world above through a reed because of a great flood. Of all the Holy People, the principal figure is Changing Woman, whose

husband is the Sun. Changing Woman bore two sons, the Hero
Twins: Monster Slayer and Child of the Water. The adventures
of the Twins provide the basis for many stories told to Navajo
children, conveying ideals for young manhood. The Hero Twins
killed most of the monsters on earth, but not all, leaving Hunger,
Poverty, Dirt, and Old Age to continue to harass mankind. Lava
is believed to be the dried blood of slain monsters. There are
many figures in Navajo mythology, including Spider Woman,
who taught the Navajos how to weave. But Changing Woman
is the most frequent subject of ceremonies and offerings, because she is the one who most consistently helps the Earth Surface People, while others are often regarded as potential sources
of harm and injury.

The Navajos have a deep-seated fear of ghosts. Any person
who dies of a cause other than old age, except an infant who has
not yet uttered a cry, produces a ghost. These ghosts return to
avenge offenses or neglect, such as an improper burial, failure
to inter the person's belongings with him, or disturbing the grave
in any way. Ghosts appear after dark, either in human form
or in the form of some dark and mysterious creature or thing:
sometimes a mouse or an owl, a coyote, or a whirlwind. Ghosts
may make bird or animal sounds or tug at people's clothes,
throw dirt at them, or chase them. A whistling in the dark is
evidence that a ghost is near. Most adult Navajos are fearful
of traveling after dark because of the possibility of confronting
a ghost. When a Navajo believes he has seen a ghost, it follows
that he or a close relative will die unless a proper ceremony is
performed. As a result of these beliefs, death is regarded as a
frightful experience. The hogan in which someone has died
is abandoned, and four days of mourning are observed after
burial in order to ensure that the spirit of the dead person can
reach the afterworld safely. There is no hopeful concept of a
life hereafter among the Navajos, only a shadowy existence
in a place beneath the earth's surface.

Witchcraft is also an important part of Navajo beliefs, although it is a subject not generally discussed with white men.
Witches are believed to inhabit the bodies of some human beings

and to have the power to produce illness or death, as well as to cast spells or cause weaknesses in human conduct. Plants and other substances are believed to provide protection against witches, and ceremonies may be performed to counteract the effect of witchcraft.

The natural outgrowth of these beliefs is a code of prohibited conduct which might be classed as superstition but which the Navajos regard quite soberly. Among the things which a Navajo will avoid are trees which have been struck by lightning. A Navajo must never kill a coyote, a bear, a snake, or certain kinds of birds. The eating of fish and of many water birds and animals is also forbidden. A melon must never be cut with the point of a knife. Navajos never comb their hair at night. They never step over someone who is lying down. Mother-in-law and son-in-law must never look into each other's eyes. This last taboo gave rise to the "mother-in-law bell," fashioned of silver and worn by Navajo mothers-in-law to alert their sons-in-law when they are approaching too close. These little bells may sometimes be found in shops where Navajo silver jewelry is sold.

A buckskin pouch is kept in most Navajo hogans, containing carved images, bits of shell and turquoise, and various charms to counteract the spells of witches or other evil forces.

It follows naturally from these beliefs that the Navajo Indians should accept the fact that illness is the result of some activity by the Holy People, or by ghosts or witches. The concept that disease might be caused by some physiological process is completely foreign to the Navajos. Disease and injury, like other misfortunes, are traced back to some violation of a rule of conduct or to the malevolent behavior of some ghost or witch, and therefore the treatment must be of the same character as the cause of the illness. If supernatural forces cause disease, supernatural means must be used to restore good health. Again it follows that the objectives of most Navajo ceremonies are either the avoidance of misfortune or the curing of illness. These ceremonies are usually performed inside the hogan, using the services of medicine men who are hired for the purpose. As in other human endeavors, the amount spent for the medicine man generally determines how elaborate the ceremony will be.

Among the principal elements of the curing ceremony are dry paintings, better known in the white man's world as "sand paintings." These paintings are done on the ground, against a background of fine sand, with pigments made from various vegetable materials such as crushed flowers, pollen, and meal. The singer and his assistants hold the grains of color in their closed hands and carefully let them run through their fingers in a fine stream as they move their hands over the background to form the pattern. There are hundreds of different designs utilized in making dry paintings, each one specially selected to fit the particular illness or disturbance of the patient. In most ceremonies at least four paintings are used, varying in size from quite small ones, which can be made by two or three people in a short period of time, to very large ones, which require large numbers of assistants. Where only part of a ceremony is given, a single painting is made, but a full performance usually calls for a painting to be made on each of four successive days. The curing ceremony usually includes the singing of chants in addition to the dry paintings, as well as some basic physical treatment such as a sweat bath or a yucca root bath. Sometimes a beverage of herbs is concocted for the patient to drink.

It is one of the ironies of reservation life that the hospital facilities provided by the Federal government are so seldom used by the Navajos. Overwhelmingly, the Navajos prefer to patronize their own medicine men in order to be cured through ceremonies. The startling fact is that in many cases this approach is as effective as the procedures used by licensed doctors. Clearly, many of the Navajo curing procedures, such as the bathing and the herb concoctions, are beneficial. Clearly also, and possibly more important, the psychological boost to the patient that comes from familiar surroundings and traditions often goes a long way toward generating an affirmative attitude which will contribute to an early cure. In the hospital setting, a Navajo may feel lonely and lost, while in his own hogan, surrounded by his fellows whom he respects and ministered to with procedures that are familiar to him, he will often respond positively.

Witchcraft and superstition serve a constructive social purpose in the Navajo culture. Witches serve as convenient scapegoats. The witch might be considered the Navajo's substitute for race prejudice. Witchcraft also serves as an economic leveler. Navajos who accumulate wealth become the subjects of gossip implying that they got their start by stealing from the dead or from some other forbidden activity. To avoid this form of envy, rich Navajos are constantly under pressure to be generous in making gifts to their relatives or neighbors in need and to spend lavishly on hospitality and on ceremonies. As a result, their accumulation of wealth is kept within reasonable bounds.

The same forces tend to keep Navajo political leaders from becoming arrogant or too powerful. The risk of being branded a witch is ever-present. Belief in witchcraft also helps to ensure proper conduct toward older people, out of a concern that neglect of the elderly may result in their resorting to witchery. Similarly, the fear of going abroad at night because of witches and ghosts has a discouraging effect on philandering males.

Intolerant white settlers often dismissed the Navajos as "cheating, stealing Indians." But the fact is that the Navajos have a strong set of values and ethics, albeit with a slightly different orientation from those of the white man. Lying and stealing are disapproved of among the Navajos, not on moral grounds but on the practical grounds of getting along well with others. In dealing with the white man, this practical need is simply not as great. The goals of the Navajos in their own setting are as fine as those of any other people. Principal stress is placed on good health and strength. Hard work and industry are highly valued, and most families rise early and work hard through the day. Skills are important as a basis for admiration but not as a means of achieving "success." In fact, the Navajos do not value success in the white man's sense. There are few Navajo millionaires; most stop accumulating wealth when they have enough to provide for family and friends, partly out of fear of being labeled witches but also because of their scale of values. Riches are not considered marks of individual achievement but rather part of a family's reward for industry. The Navajos tend to think in terms of the group rather than of the individual, and few individuals among them will presume to serve as spokesmen for the group. Indeed, one of the early sources of white-Indian conflict was the white man's belief that the Indians had violated treaties which had been made with individual leaders and by which the tribes at large did not feel bound. The qualities of character most highly prized by the Navajos are dependability, helpfulness, generosity, productiveness, and the ability to get along with others; those most strongly disapproved of are cruelty, destructiveness, laziness, and stinginess.

The Navajo people are particularly respectful of nature, which they regard as more powerful than man. They respect the integrity of the individual, but they also recognize that human nature is a blend of both good and evil, which combine to form the whole personality. Above all, the Navajos, being conscious of the dangers of life, put great emphasis on maintaining orderliness in matters which can be controlled by human activity. They have a natural distrust of strangers, avoid excesses, and generally greet each new situation by sitting back and doing nothing until sure of the right way to move.

Navajo standards of justice are most instructive. Highest on the Navajo list of crimes are witchcraft and incest. Crimes of violence, such as assault, rape, and murder, are punished more by compensation to the victim or his family than by retribution or revenge. A donation of livestock to the relatives of a murder victim, or payment to compensate for economic loss, are much more acceptable to the Navajos than the concepts of the white man's justice.

In the eyes of the Navajo, the white man is a temporary conqueror who must be dealt with today but may be gone tomorrow. A visitor should not expect to find a warm welcome, but he will find civility. Long and bitter experience has taught the Navajo to distrust the white man, and this is fully understandable. But by visiting the Navajo in his home setting—with the opportunity to explore Canyon de Chelly, to admire the Navajo's handiwork, his flocks, his farming methods—one can begin to understand him. And with some quiet time for reflection, one might also philosophize about the differences in outlook between the two races and the challenge to our own values. Is the Navajo view of moderation less admirable than the white man's view of success? Is the Navajo's concern about witches more ignorant than our own prejudice against minorities? Is the Navajo's respect for nature less sensible than our programs of exploitation? Is the Navajo's tradition of generosity and family life less desirable than our concentration on individual achievement and wealth?

THE HOPIS

It is sometimes said that a visit to a Southwest Indian reservation is like studying living archaeology. If there is any one Indian tribe that fits that definition it is the Hopis, a group of over 5,000 Pueblo Indians who have lived on three mesas in the Arizona desert for hundreds of years with virtually no change in their traditions or life style. Visiting the Hopi mesas is like being transported backward in time. There are some evidences of modern "civilization," such as trucks, canned goods, and a few telephones, but the basic pattern and structure of Hopi life have not changed for centuries.

The Hopi villages are perched on the tops and slopes of high mesas. Having originally been so placed for security, they have served to insulate this hardy people from the invasions of other peoples and other cultures. The villages look parched and bleak at first glance, but they house a proud people and a colorful tradition. The Hopis are an agricultural people, growing mainly beans, squash, and corn. They are also known for their distinctive handicraft. The tribe is organized into clans. Real property is held by the women and is passed on from mother to daughter through the generations. The Spanish visited the Hopi villages on several occasions between 1540 to 1680, bringing with them livestock and fruit trees. Interestingly, in the Hopi villages today, the livestock is owned by the men—in the Spanish tradition—and not by the women, as is other tribal property. During the Pueblo Indian uprising in 1680, the Hopis destroyed the Spanish missions and killed the priests. Thereafter the Spanish never again attempted to conquer this tough people. Even as the white pioneers and settlers expanded southward and westward, the Hopis kept to themselves and were largely undisturbed by the military expeditions of the nineteenth century.

There are today eleven Hopi villages, most of them situated atop mesas. Each village is autonomous, keeps its own lands, and has its own government, although the Federal government has attempted to impose a single structure and tribal council to manage the affairs of all of the villages. Despite this effort, tribal solidarity within each village continues to assert itself, maintaining its individual character, as in the old Greek city-states, with no feeling of unity throughout.

The Hopi reservation is located in the middle of the larger Navajo reservation which surrounds it, and most of the Hopi villages are connected by an all-weather road which runs from east to west. As one comes to them, going from east to west, the villages are called by the following descriptive names: On First Mesa—Hano ("Eastern people"), Sichomovi ("Place of the mound where wild currants grow"), and Walpi ("Place of the gap"); on Second Mesa—Shungopovi ("Place by the spring where the tall reeds grow"), Mishongnovi ("Place of the black man"), and Shipaulovi ("Where the mosquitoes are"); on Third Mesa—Kiakochomovi ("Place of the hills of ruins," also known as New Oraibi), Oraibi ("Place of the rock called orai"), Hotevilla ("Skinned back"), Bakabi ("Place of the jointed reeds"), and, 35 miles to the west, Moenkopi ("Place of running water"). The oldest of these villages is Oraibi, which is believed to have been founded about A.D. 1150 by a group which had previously lived on Second Mesa. In 1906, following a factional split caused by the policies of the United States Bureau of Indian Affairs, a substantial part of Oraibi's population left to found a new village at Hotevilla where they could practice their religion without interference. The present-day residents of Hotevilla still maintain a sturdy independence from Federal government policies.

Despite some modern conveniences, many of the old practices and customs still thrive in the Hopi villages. One of these is the

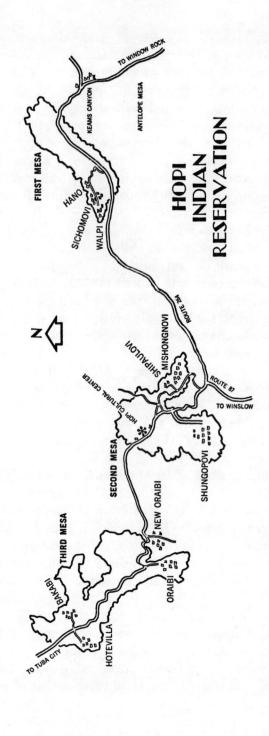

HOPI
INDIAN
RESERVATION

FIRST MESA
HANO
SICHOMOVI
WALPI
KEAMS CANYON
TO WINDOW ROCK
ANTELOPE MESA

N

ROUTE 264
MISHONGNOVI
SHIPAULOVI
ROUTE 87
TO WINSLOW
SHUNGOPOVI
HOPI CULTURAL CENTER

SECOND MESA
NEW ORAIBI
ORAIBI

THIRD MESA
BAKABI
HOTEVILLA
TO TUBA CITY

baking of "piki," a very thin bread now made primarily for use during religious ceremonial periods but still produced in accordance with the painstaking tradition that has been handed down over many generations. The procedure followed today is almost exactly the same as that described a century ago by Major John Wesley Powell, the explorer who scouted the Grand Canyon and the surrounding territory. This is Major Powell's description:

> In the corner of the house is a little oven, the top of which is a great flat stone, and the good housewife bakes her bread in this manner: The corn meal is mixed to the consistency of a rather thick gruel, and the woman dips her hand into the mixture and plasters the hot stone with a thin coating of the meal paste. In a minute or two it forms into a thin paperlike cake, and she takes it up by the edge, folds it once, and places it on a basket tray; then another and another sheet of paper-bread is made in like manner and piled on the tray. I notice that the paste stands in a number of different bowls and that she takes from one bowl and then another in order, and I soon see the effect of this. The corn before being ground is assorted by colors, white, yellow, red, blue, and black, and the sheets of bread, when made, are of the same variety of colors, white, yellow, red, blue, and black. This bread, held on very beautiful trays, is itself a work of art. They call it piki.

The Hopi inheritance of folklore and mythology is probably the richest in the Southwest. Elaborate ceremonies occur throughout the year, and the traditional religious practices are fiercely maintained. The basic objectives of the rites are fertility, long life, healing, and rain. During the first half of the year—from the time of the winter solstice through July—the ceremonies are performed by dancers wearing kachina masks representing those kachinas who take part in the particular ceremony. The kachinas themselves are not worshiped as gods but are thought of, rather, as supernatural beings or spirits which symbolize many different animal and human qualities. They live, according to Hopi belief, on the San Francisco Peaks which rise beyond the mesas, and they visit the Hopi villages for half of each year. They dance, they sing, they bring presents to the Hopi children, and most important they bring the rain. There are hundreds of different kachinas. Some are considered to be kindly and helpful beings. Others are ogres whose function is to scare or punish those who break rules of religious or social conduct. Still others perform the function of clowns and provide amusement and a light touch to otherwise serious ceremonies. When a dancer puts on the mask and costume of a kachina and applies paint to his body in the traditional designs, the Hopi people believe that he actually becomes the kachina he is impersonating. The dancers who impersonate the kachinas are always men, even though the character impersonated may be female.

Before a kachina ceremony, the men of the village carve from cottonwood root small replicas of the various figures which will take part in the dance. During the ceremony these kachina dolls are given to the Hopi children for them to take home as reminders of the kachinas all through the year. The dolls decorate the walls and rafters of Hopi homes and serve to educate the young in the tribal traditions. In more recent years, the dolls are also made for the tourist trade and may be found in shops and trading posts throughout the Southwest. They range in size from a few inches to almost two feet tall, and also range in quality of workmanship from lathe-turned pieces to hand-carved and beautifully painted authentic dolls.

The major ceremonies of the Hopi Indians' year present a fascinating sequence. In November there is an annual initiation ceremony, called Wuwuchim, during which all roads and trails leading into the village are sealed off with sacred meal to prevent outsiders from coming in. During this ceremony the emergence of the people from the underworld is re-enacted.

A winter solstice ceremony, called Soyal, is held in December, the purpose of which is to bring back the sun from its northward journey and to mark the start of a new year. Soyal marks the beginning of the season for kachina ceremonies. The first major ceremony of the kachina season is the Bean Dance, called Powamu, in which a great number and variety of kachina performers participate. During this ceremony the ugly kachinas visit the homes of naughty children to help instill a spirit of good behavior, with threats to devour the youngsters if they do not behave. The sight of these ogres is enough to impress anyone, even the boldest of bad boys. During the same season, the Water Serpent ceremony, Palolokon, is performed to honor the serpents who control the waters and to ensure that they will provide the water necessary to keep the springs flowing and to nourish the new crops.

One of the gayer kachina dances is Niman, the Home Dance, a sixteen-day ceremony that ends in July and marks the final kachina ceremony of the year. This dance includes a number of clowns who give comic relief in between the more formal dances, sometimes mimicking the behavior of uncouth guests. Niman usually coincides with the early harvest, and corn and melons are often distributed, along with piki and other native foods. Dolls, bows and arrows, rattles, and other gifts are given to the children.

The Hopi ceremony most widely known by outsiders is the Snake Dance, which features live snakes held in the dancers' mouths. The Snake Dance and the Flute Ceremony alternate annually at the end of each August. The Snake Dance culminates a sixteen-day ceremony and derives from the legend of a young man who attempted to find the source of all waters. He eventually found the great snake who controls the waters of the world. The young Indian was initiated into the snake tribe and married a girl who had been transformed into a snake. Their progeny are believed to be all of the snakes which now inhabit the world. The young man was subsequently designated as Antelope Chief by the Spider Woman (a figure which also appears in Navajo beliefs) and was sent to teach the ceremonies of the snake people to the Hopi people so that they could avoid droughts. Before the Snake Dance, it is required that snakes be gathered from the surrounding countryside over the course of four days. All of the snakes that are found are brought into the kivas where the Snake and Antelope societies conduct religious rites. The snakes are washed and blessed. On the day of the dance, a foot race is held at dawn. The runners make their way down the trail which leads off the mesa to the flat plain and a watercourse below and then race back to the foot of the mesa and up its steep slope, bearing a container of water for the kiva. Following this, a children's race is run on the mesa top by the boys and girls of the village, who carry green stalks of corn. Later in the day, the formal Snake Dance takes place in the village plaza. A dancer takes up one of the snakes which has been blessed and puts it in his mouth, holding it firmly a few inches behind the head. A second dancer distracts the snake with a stick which has eagle feathers tied to its tip. Another dancer takes up a snake, and so it continues until all of the snakes are carried by dancers. At the end of the dance the snakes are placed in a circle ringed with cornmeal. Then the snake men pick them up and race down the mesa to free them so they can act as messengers to carry the prayers for rain to the spirits of the waters.

Although visitors have been permitted to attend the outdoor parts of many of these ceremonies in past years, there is a growing tendency to exclude them in order to preserve the integrity and dignity of the ceremony.

THE RIO GRANDE PUEBLO INDIANS

In a country that prides itself on religious freedom and toleration, the treatment of American Indians has been one of intolerance and religious oppression from the time the white man first set foot on Indian lands. Missionaries have repeatedly tried to snuff out "pagan" beliefs and save Indian souls by imposing Christianity on the "uncivilized savage." It is a tribute to the fortitude of the Southwest Indians that they have managed to preserve as much as they have of their own religious convictions in the face of so much interference and well-intentioned oppression.

The Pueblo Indians of the Rio Grande in New Mexico present a dramatic example of how the Indians have managed to survive in a world in which religious ideas have been imposed upon them. From the very first visit by Coronado in 1540, the Spanish made it a primary objective of their colonial efforts in the Southwest to convert Indians to Christianity. Franciscan missions were constructed throughout the territory, and the friars frequently wielded far greater power than the civil governors. The Indians revolted occasionally, and the killing of priests was not unsual, but the incessant drive to save Indian souls kept pushing on. The results may be seen in the Pueblo communities along the Rio Grande today, communities which were primary targets of conversion by the Spanish for 300 years. Although most Pueblo Indians today are baptized, confirmed, and married by Catholic priests, they continue also to cling to their own traditional religious ceremonies and participate in many ancient native rites. Where there has been complete conversion of the Indians to Christianity, factionalism has developed and frequently bloodshed has followed. Generally, however, the history of religious intolerance has been one of accommodation. The Indians have good-naturedly accepted some of the white man's medicine while at the same time keeping their own traditions. The ceremonial dances which take place in the Rio Grande pueblos today are often scheduled to be held on saints' days. A ceremony usually begins with a mass in the church. When the mass is over, the Indian spiritual leaders sound a drum and emerge from the kiva to conduct the second stage of the proceedings. The saint's statue is usually carried out from the church and placed on a stand in the plaza, around which the Indians dance, frequently kissing the robe of the patron saint before retiring to the kiva. Such polyglot ceremonies cover all bases, combining a Christian religious service with a Corn Dance or Rain Dance to placate the gods who control natural forces. The result is both whimsical and sad.

The kiva is a major cultural and religious institution of the Pueblo Indians. It is the religious temple for purposes of ceremony, but it also serves as a meeting place for the menfolk. Each clan has its own kiva, which is usually entered through a hole in the roof from which a ladder protrudes. The room below is round, with sitting benches around the walls and a small hole in the floor to represent the space through which the people originally emerged from the underworld. This unique institution continues to play an important part in the lives of the Pueblo Indians, not only along the Rio Grande but also among the Hopis and the Zuñis.

The Pueblo Indians of today are the successors to the cliff dwellers who once occupied places like Mesa Verde and Bandelier. Many of their traditions and cultural patterns remain unchanged after hundreds of years, but others have given way to modern civilization. The major Pueblo community at Taos, most northerly of the group along the Rio Grande, pretty well exemplifies the changes that have been taking place everywhere among the Pueblo Indians. There are two large adobe communal houses at Taos, four and five stories in height. Originally, the only means of entrance to these structures was by way of ladders leading down from hatchways in the roofs. But by the end of the nineteenth century, when danger of enemy attack had largely disappeared, doors and windows were cut into the adobe walls. Ladders are still used to climb to the upper stories since there are no inside staircases. In addition to the principal residential structures, there are also smaller buildings and platforms used to store grain. Small round baking ovens can be seen near the houses, and so can the upper ends of the ladders which portrude from the entrances to underground kivas. The women are the heads of the families, and the men work as farmers or at nearby jobs. Taos parents teach their children the tribal traditions and ceremonies at an early age, in an attempt to guard them against contamination by white civilization. Much of the effect of this is lost through the ever-present hordes of tourists who come to Taos in increasing numbers, although an effort is made to contain them in the public spaces in order to preserve a semblance of privacy in the other parts of the Pueblo.

There are a number of interesting Pueblo Indian villages ranging across northern New Mexico, from Acoma on the west to Taos on the east. Many of these villages can be visited, provided that basic rules of good conduct and good sense are followed. Some charge parking or admissions fees. Many have ceremonies to which the public is admitted. The most interesting follow.

Acoma Pueblo is sometimes called the Sky City because of its

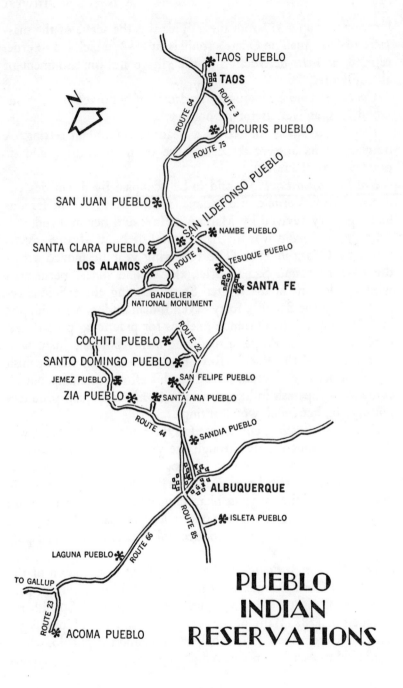

TAOS PUEBLO

TAOS

ROUTE 64

ROUTE 3

PICURIS PUEBLO

ROUTE 75

SAN JUAN PUEBLO

SAN ILDEFONSO PUEBLO

NAMBE PUEBLO

SANTA CLARA PUEBLO

ROUTE 4

TESUQUE PUEBLO

LOS ALAMOS

SANTA FE

BANDELIER
NATIONAL MONUMENT

COCHITI PUEBLO

ROUTE 22

SANTO DOMINGO PUEBLO

JEMEZ PUEBLO

SAN FELIPE PUEBLO

ZIA PUEBLO

SANTA ANA PUEBLO

ROUTE 44

SANDIA PUEBLO

ALBUQUERQUE

ISLETA PUEBLO

ROUTE 66

ROUTE 85

LAGUNA PUEBLO

TO GALLUP

ROUTE 23

ACOMA PUEBLO

PUEBLO
INDIAN
RESERVATIONS

location on top a 357-foot mesa. This was the scene of the massacre of Don Juan de Oñate's soldiers in 1598, which led to cruel reprisals and the destruction of the village and imprisonment of all survivors.

Cochiti Pueblo is famous for its drums of hollowed-out cottonwood logs, as well as for its pottery.

Picuris Pueblo is located in a beautiful mountain setting. A number of its ancient structures are open to visitors, and its pottery is well known.

San Ildefonso Pueblo is said to be occupied by direct descendants of Mesa Verde cliff dwellers. It is the source of the famous black pottery revived by Maria Martínez and her husband.

San Juan Pueblo was the first capital of New Mexico, established by Oñate in 1598. The following year he moved across the river to found San Gabriel, the second oldest permanent white settlement in the United States. During the religious repressions by the Spanish, forty-seven Indian leaders were shipped in 1675 from the Rio Grande pueblos for practicing pagan rites. One of these was Po-pé, a medicine man from San Juan, who later organized the Pueblo Revolt of 1680 against the Spanish and then became a tyrant himself in his efforts to stamp out all evidence of Spanish influence on Indian life. San Juan produces pottery, baskets, and woodcarvings.

Santa Clara Pueblo, constructed in the fourteenth century, was the scene of much strife through the years in the effort to preserve ancient ways in the face of progress. Currently the pueblo operates under a tribal constitution which leaves ceremonial life in the hands of the religious hierarchy, while secular matters are handled by younger, more modern leaders. Santa Clara has a number of craftsmen who produce polished red and black pottery.

Santo Domingo Pueblo is the scene of the best known of the ceremonial Corn Dances. This pueblo played an important part in the revolt of 1680 and was destroyed during the Spanish reconquest of 1782. Many of the survivors escaped to Hopi villages where they remained. Others helped to rebuild the pueblo, which continued to carry on native religious practices in secret, nurturing the strong tradition which continues to the present time. Santo Domingo is well known for its turquoise and shell jewelry.

Taos Pueblo is the most popular and the most photographed of the pueblos because of its multistoried structures.

Zia Pueblo has been the scene of bloodshed and strife throughout its history. An active participant in the Pueblo rebellion, Zia was subjected to a fierce attack by the Spanish in 1689. More than six hundred of its inhabitants were killed and the town was destroyed. Captives were sold into slavery. When the survivors returned to re-establish the Pueblo after 1692, they decided to ally themselves with the Spanish, only to find that other Indian tribes resented this arrangement and subjected them to frequent raids. Recent internal disagreements led to the burning of a kiva only a few years ago.

The symbol of authority for Pueblo Indian leaders has been a rod, or cane, since the arrival of Oñate in 1598. The Spaniards required each pueblo to select a governor whose authority would be represented by his rod of office. After the American occupation, President Abraham Lincoln presented ebony canes with silver handles to each of the pueblo governors in 1863. Many of these Lincoln canes are still in existence and used by the head men of the pueblos.

THE ZUÑIS

Zuñi is the community which Coronado attacked in 1540, believing it to be one of the Seven Cities of Cíbola, where fabled golden treasure was to be found. Dislike of the Spanish has continued to this day, as the result of the treatment received by the Zuñi people from Coronado and other conquerors during the 300-year Spanish occupation.

Today, instead of golden treasure, Zuñi pottery is well known throughout the Southwest, and still better known is the beautiful work done by the Zuñi silversmiths, who have developed an original inlay technique called channel work. Zuñi jewelry, largely silver and turquoise, is highly prized.

The Zuñi Pueblo today still keeps its own distinctive culture,

language, and religion. Because of its remoteness from other
Spanish-dominated pueblos, Zuñi was better able to preserve the
integrity of its religious practices and customs than its neighbors
to the east and north.

For good or ill, the march of civilization has now begun
to make its mark on Zuñi. Gas stations and various commercial
structures have become evident in the heart of the village, as well
as an increasing number of modern houses with the most up-to-
date conveniences. Nonetheless the Zuñi Indians have a great
treasure in their traditions and myths.

Zuñi folk tales are many and charming, and a number have
been translated into English and published in collections. One
of the loveliest legends is the story of the Corn Maidens. The
God of Dawn one day presented to the people of Zuñi seven
corn plants growing in their dance court, with seven lovely
maidens standing nearby. As the people chanted prayers of
thanksgiving, the maidens danced and motioned the corn upward
with their magic wands, so that the people might have corn and
plenty. Irreverence and ingratitude soon raised their ugly heads,
however, and some of the young men began to covet the maidens
and pluck at their garments as they danced. Displeased, the
Dawn God called his daughters back to his house in the rainbow
and decreed that the people must experience want. Years of trial
and famine followed. The young men went out to search for
the lost maidens. Finally, four youths were sent to the land of
summer, where they found the God of Dawn and the Corn
Maidens. After making the proper offerings, the youths were
given the growing plants containing the substance of the maidens'
flesh to bring back to the Zuñi people, who to this day hold seed
corn sacred.

The religion of the Zuñi people is inseparably intertwined
with their daily lives. There are six religious "divisions," each
with its own kiva and each representing a direction. In order of
precedence, they are North, West, South, East, High, and Low.
Each kiva is associated with an animal symbol and a color: the
mountain lion and yellow for North, the bear and blue for West,
the badger and red for South, the wolf and white for East, the

eagle and the "many hues of the sky" for High, and the mole
and black for Low. As in the other pueblo communities, mem-
bership in the kivas is restricted to men only, and the boys are
initiated when they are still quite young.

Ceremonies follow one another logically throughout the Zuñi
year, starting with the New Year's activities which take place
following the winter solstice—usually in early January. They
all lead up to the most important ceremony of the year, the
Shalako, which comes in late November or early December. In
this ceremony, dancers representing gods re-enact the creation
of the Zuñi people and their migration to the "Middle Place."
They bless the houses which have been built in their honor and
offer prayers for the people's long, happy, and prosperous lives
and for bountiful harvests and fertility. At the time of the New
Year, the dance participants are chosen and families are assigned
the responsibility of building several houses to receive the gods.
A number of figures in the ceremony, including that of the
Shalako god, are represented by members of each of the six kivas.
Certain other figures are represented by members of certain kivas
only. The six Shalako god impersonators stand about ten feet
tall when in costume on Shalako day. They carry their masks
and their embroidered garments on long poles, the garments
being held out from their bodies by hoops, like those of an old-
fashioned hoop skirt. The Shalako mask is turquoise in color. It
has two horns curving up from either side, two large round eyes,
and what appears to be a long beak extending from the center
of the face. The beak is fashioned from two pieces of wood
which make a loud clapping noise when handled properly by
the dancer. The mask is crowned with a fan-shaped headdress of
eagle feathers and finished off at the neck with a ruff made from
shorter, darker feathers. The full effect of these tall figures is
spectacular. The other dancers in the Shalako ceremony remain
in human scale.

After the dancers are appointed, they must spend long hours
and many weeks learning their chants and performing the various religious rites required of them. They are also expected to
help with the building of the Shalako houses. All of this prepara-

tion leaves them no time for other work, and so it is the duty of the families who are chosen for the honor to see that they are well fed and cared for throughout the year. With the arrival of fall comes an increase in the frequency of religious ceremonies and a bustling air of activity about the whole village. The houses and yards are cleaned up, and the women of the village cook and bake full-time. At last comes Shalako day, a full day and night of ceremony, dancing, and feasting. The ceremony actually begins on the afternoon of one day and is completed by the afternoon of the following day. Many different and age-old rituals are observed. The impersonators of the gods come, at dusk, in a procession from far across the fields to the village. There, all through the night, they perform their chants, they dance, they bless the houses which have been built in their honor. In the morning they rest awhile, and by noon they have formed their procession and are on their way back across the fields to the distant place from which they came. And the Zuñi people are blessed for another year.

THE UTES

Of all the Indian reservations in the Southwest, none is more depressing than Ute Mountain in the southwest corner of Colorado. The once great Ute Indians, the only indigenous tribe in Colorado, formerly hunted in the mountains and on the plains of both Utah and Colorado and represented a fierce and proud tradition. Agreeing to accept reservation life in the nineteenth century, they were betrayed by government representatives who permitted prospectors to violate their territorial limits, finally precipitating the Ute uprising which gave a colorable excuse for moving the Utes out of Colorado almost entirely.

The once-great Ute name, memorialized in the name of the state of Utah, has been slowly but surely eroded. Much of the land on which the Utes were relocated was distributed as individual lots in an attempt to "civilize" the members of the tribe by teaching them the European concept of individual property rights. White men were permitted to homestead the lots not occupied by the Indians, and eventually most of the land originally assigned for Ute occupancy was acquired by white homesteaders. Many of the lots owned by the Indians were bought up by speculators with ready cash to offer in exchange. In 1950, the Ute tribe won a $31-million judgment from the United States government because of its land claims. But money is no sub stitute for homeland and tradition. The modern Ute Indian is a sad reflection of his old self. Most of the southern Utes speak English and dress like white people. They live in development houses in a community which looks like a run-down suburb of a large city. Most of the traditional ceremonies have disappeared. A visit to the Ute Mountain Indian reservation is worthwhile principally for the picture it presents of the corruption of native traditions by white civilization. A combination of this visit with a trip to the Ute Indian Museum near Montrose, Colorado, one of the finest displays of a tribe's history anywhere in the Southwest, gives poignant emphasis to the impact of the white man on the Indian.

PART TWO
Places to Visit

7
Planning Your Trip

Yogi Berra, of New York Yankee fame, once took a friend to an Italian restaurant which Berra had praised highly in advance. When Berra and his friend arrived at the place, they found it packed with people. There was a long waiting line. Berra remarked to his friend in disgust, as they turned to leave, "No wonder no one comes here anymore. It's too crowded."

The same might be said about the Grand Canyon. Once a place where people could sense awesome isolation as they viewed one of the extraordinary marvels of nature, the Grand Canyon's existing facilities for visitors are now too crowded for real enjoyment. During the summer, the time when most families are able to take a vacation, the campgrounds are quickly filled, and with more than their share of off-beat types who have come for the companionship of the place rather than for its natural beauty. On the North Rim, once an idyllic spot because of its relative difficulty of access, the campground is usually full by 11 A.M. Later arrivals, who have driven many miles through completely unpopulated terrain, are confronted by this discouraging sign:

CAMPGROUND FULL.
NEAREST CAMPGROUND 44 MILES NORTH AT
JACOB LAKE.

135

New tactics are necessary for real enjoyment in visiting the Southwest. Those who are genuinely interested in enjoying the wonders of the region should concentrate on the park areas off the beaten track. The Grand Canyon has to be seen once, but it need not be the focal point of your trip. Indeed, if one wishes to see it truly—after an initial visit and glimpses from lookouts around the rim—one should go back for several days at an uncrowded time of the year and take the time to go down into the canyon. For purposes of a summer vacation visit, however, perhaps the best way to get some feeling for the Grand Canyon is to plan the better part of a day here, leaving camping gear behind, getting an early morning start by automobile—heading for either the North or South Rim—exploring the various lookouts and vistas into the canyon, and returning to camp by nightfall.

In contrast to places like Capitol Reef National Park, which few people know about and even fewer visit, the rock ledges of Bright Angel Point at the Grand Canyon are likely to be draped with kibitzers whose chief pleasure in being there seems to be outdoing each other in the cleverness of their remarks about other visitors who come to see the view. The view should still be seen, notwithstanding these distractions, but it is difficult to concentrate on the larger significance of the canyon's grandeur when evidences of today's civilization are pressing in on all sides. If you should decide to drive to the North Rim, incidentally, be sure to take the side road out to Cape Royal. The view from Angel's Window, which affords a glimpse of the river, is breathtaking. There are several other overlooks along this road which also merit a stop, and if you return toward evening the chances are very good that you will spot some deer along the way.

Many of the things that can be said about the Grand Canyon apply also, although to a lesser degree, to Bryce Canyon National Park in Utah. The pink cliffs and spires are unusual phenomena of nature, but, taken together with other places to be seen in the area, they hardly seem to merit the masses of people who crowd the park to "ooh" and "ah." Most of the overlooks are fenced in with railings and interpretive signs, a practical necessity but also a feature which diminishes one's sense of the natural setting. The campground is often full and the general atmosphere of the visitors' center and other facilities is somewhat frantic. Unless one has a burning desire to touch all bases, one could well plan

Bryce Canyon National Park

a trip to the Southwest which avoided Bryce entirely or else included a visit of only a few hours. In case of an overnight stay, one worthwhile excursion is the 8:00 A.M. horseback ride down the canyon trail. A large number of horses and mules are usually included on the trip, so that it lacks a certain personal quality, but nonetheless the experience is unusual and at times exciting.

Petrified Forest National Park in Arizona, which includes the Painted Desert, also falls into the category of a facility which is too crowded. Nonetheless it does include some natural features which are striking and unusual, and if one's route passes that way it would be unfortunate to miss it. The park is seen simply by driving through from one end to the other. There are no camping facilities and, in fact, all visitors are chased out by nightfall to prevent illicit taking of specimens. The park can be entered from the north end (on Interstate 40) or from the south (on U.S. 180), depending on which way one is traveling. The most striking collection of petrified logs is located near the southern entrance to the park, in the area of the museum. The museum, incidentally, contains first-rate interpretive exhibits ex-

plaining how the agatized wood came into being. It also contains
an amusing display of specimens returned by visitors who pur-
loined them, together with letters expressing the pangs of con-
science which prompted their return. Despite the interesting
psychological insights of this particular display, the over-all emphasis on the the prohibition of specimen collecting and the dire
consequences to those who would remove pieces of petrified
wood from the park rather spoils the atmosphere of a visit.
Everyone is presumed to be a thief in the eyes of the admin-
istrators. Within the park, Blue Mesa is worth a side journey.
It illustrates a stage of desolate erosion which must be similar
to the surface of the moon. The same desolation, although more
colorful, exists in the Painted Desert end of the park, which is
viewed from several drive-off parking places. One special feature
of Petrified Forest National Park is the excellent gift shop in the
visitors' center at the Painted Desert entrance. (While the museum display presents the scientific explanation of the Petrified
Forest's genesis, there is another explanation found in Indian
legend. It is said that once, long ago, there was a goddess who
came to this place hungry and exhausted. She killed a rabbit
with a club and then tried to build a fire to cook it with some of
the logs which were lying about on the ground. Finding the
logs too wet to burn, the hungry goddess, in her anger and
frustration, cursed the spot and turned the logs to stone so that
they might never be used to build a fire.)

Having thus dealt with the three or four best-known natural
features of the Southwest, to which tourists flock in droves each
year, let us turn now to the part of the Southwest where one
can really enjoy a visit. The principal area to which this book
relates is the Colorado Plateau, consisting of the southern portions of Utah and Colorado and the northern portions of Arizona
and New Mexico. In the next chapters of the book there are
individual descriptions of ten interesting and beautiful areas
which are, so far, reasonably unspoiled. But one should not as-
sume that this is the extent of the places worth visiting in the
Southwest. Far from it. There are countless natural areas open
to visitors, many of them far less developed than those described

hereafter. This book is intended only as an introduction to whet the appetite, not as a definitive description of all of the places it is possible to visit. If your interest is stimulated enough to plan a trip to the Southwest, the purpose of the book has been served. Planning the details of the trip is part of the fun, and you should spend some time working out a plan for your visit which has its own special individuality. It is hoped that this book will provide, simply, a good starting point.

The general theory expounded here of a visit to the Southwest is to camp out of doors and to plan to spend between one and three days (or more if you can) at the places that appeal to you. The time goes quickly, between attending to the house-keeping details which are necessary on any camping expedition and getting around to see everything you can. A morning can be spent on a walk, an afternoon taking pictures or sketching, and the day has slipped by. Although some places can be enjoyed with just a few hours spent late one afternoon and early the next morning, it is best to avoid too much frantic moving from one spot to another, night after night. It makes more sense to give up visits to certain areas and allow yourself enough time to enjoy fully those places you do visit.

For a start on the planning process, there follows a list of the national parks and monuments in the area of the Southwest to which this book relates. The descriptions have been prepared by the National Park Service, and the list is arranged alphabetically by state. After each description there is a mailing address. If a description intrigues you, send a letter or postcard to the mailing address and ask for a folder, which will provide enough details for you to make intelligent planning decisions. Areas followed by a chapter reference are described in more detail later.

ARIZONA

Canyon de Chelly National Monument (Chapter 10)
Prehistoric Indian ruins in dramatic setting at the base of sheer red cliffs and in caves in canyon walls; modern Navajo Indian homes and farms.
Notes: Guided tours, camping, horseback riding; lodging and food

in park; elevation 5,538–7,500 feet.
Address: Box 588, Chinle, Ariz. 86503.

Grand Canyon National Monument
Part of the Grand Canyon of the Colorado River containing Toro-
weap Point, with its striking view of the Inner Gorge.
Notes: Camping, hiking; elevation 7,700 feet.
Address: Box 129, Grand Canyon, Ariz. 86023.

Grand Canyon National Park
Most spectacular part of the Colorado River's greatest canyon,
which is 217 miles long and 4 to 18 miles wide; rocks representing
vast span of geologic time.
Notes: Guided tours, camping, hiking, horseback riding, fishing
(North Rim closed in winter); lodging and food in park; elevation
7,000–9,100 feet.
Address: Box 129, Grand Canyon, Ariz. 86023.

Hubbell Trading Post National Historic Site (Chapter 17)
Preserves perhaps the finest example of an extant Indian trading post,
where an important story of Indian-white acculturation is told.
Notes: Guided tours; food near park.
Address: Box 388, Ganado, Ariz. 86505.

Montezuma Castle National Monument
One of the best-preserved cliff dwellings in the United States; orig-
inal five-story, twenty-room structure is 90 percent intact.
Notes: Guided tours; lodging and food near park.
Address: Box 218, Camp Verde, Ariz. 86322.

Navajo National Monument
Three large and elaborate cliff dwellings, in impressive setting, which
were abandoned more than six centuries ago.
Notes: Guided tours, camping, hiking, horseback riding; elevation
7,300 feet.
Address: Tonalea, Ariz. 86044.

Petrified Forest National Park
Probably the greatest display of petrified wood known in the world;
includes the most colorful parts of the Painted Desert.
Notes: Hiking, food in park; elevation 5,600 feet.
Address: Holbrook, Ariz. 86025.

Pipe Spring National Monument
Historic fort and other structures built by Mormon pioneers. Memorializes the struggle for settlement of part of the Southwest.
Notes: Guided tours; elevation 5,000 feet.
Address: c/o Zion National Park, Springdale, Utah 84767.

Sunset Crater National Monument
A recent volcanic cinder cone formed by an eruption in A.D. 1065. Upper part colored as if by sunset glow.
Notes: Hiking; elevation 7,000 feet.
Address: c/o Wupatki National Monument, Tuba Star Route, Flagstaff, Ariz. 86001.

Tuzigoot National Monument
Excavated ruins of a prehistoric town that was built by Indians who farmed the Verde Valley between A.D. 1125 and 1400.
Notes: Guided tours; lodging and food near park.
Address: Box 68, Clarkdale, Ariz. 86324.

Walnut Canyon National Monument
Cliff dwellings built by the Sinagua Indians in the early 1100's, in a setting of surpassing beauty.
Notes: Guided tours; lodging and food near park; elevation 6,690 feet.
Address: Route 1, Box 790, Flagstaff, Ariz. 86001.

Wupatki National Monument
Remains of prehistoric villages built by farming Indians on land enriched by ash and cinders spewed from the Sunset Crater eruption of A.D. 1065. (See Sunset Crater National Monument.)
Address: Tuba Star Route, Flagstaff, Ariz. 86001.

COLORADO

Black Canyon of the Gunnison National Monument
Spectacular Gunnison River Gorge, notable for its narrowness, depth, ruggedness, and great expanses of sheer walls; its shadowed depth accentuates dark, ancient rocks of obscure origin.
Notes: Camping, hiking.
Address: 334 South 10th Street, Montrose, Colo. 81401.

Colorado National Monument
Colorful, spectacular erosional forms—massive ramparts, sheer-walled canyons, and delicately sculptured monoliths and spires.
Notes: Camping, hiking.
Address: 334 South 10th Street, Montrose, Colo. 81401.

Great Sand Dunes National Monument (Chapter 14)
Winds blowing across the San Luis Valley for countless centuries have deposited sand dunes, 600 feet high, at the base of the lofty Sangre de Cristo Mountains.
Notes: Guided tours, camping, hiking; food near park; elevation 7,600–9,800 feet.
Address: Box 60, Alamosa, Colo. 81101.

Hovenweep National Monument
Ruins of six impressive groups of prehistoric towers, pueblos, and cliff dwellings in the desolate country north of the San Juan River. Approach roads are only fair in good weather and very difficult following storms.
Notes: Camping; elevation 5,200 feet.
Address: c/o Mesa Verde National Park, Mesa Verde, Colo. 81330.

Mesa Verde National Park (Chapter 15)
Most widely known and among the best preserved cliff dwellings and other works of prehistoric man in the United States.
Notes: Guided tours, camping, hiking, horseback riding; lodging and food in park; elevation 6,970 feet.
Address: Mesa Verde National Park, Colo. 81330.

NEW MEXICO

Aztec Ruins National Monument
Ruins of a great prehistoric Indian town built of masonry and timber during the 1100's, largely excavated and stabilized.
Notes: Guided tours; lodging and food near park; elevation 5,600 feet.
Address: Route 1, Box 101, Aztec, N.M. 87410.

Bandelier National Monument (Chapter 9)
Prehistoric Indian homes of the later Pueblo Period, in large scenic area that has more than 60 miles of back-country trails.

Notes: Guided tours, camping; lodging and food in park; elevation 6,066–8,182 feet.
Address: Los Alamos, N.M. 87544.

Chaco Canyon National Monument
Twelve major Indian ruins and more than 300 smaller archaeological sites, representing highest point of Pueblo prehistoric civilization. Unpaved approach road.
Notes: Guided tours, camping; elevation 6,300 feet.
Address: Box 156, Bloomfield, N.M. 87413.

El Morro National Monument
Inscription Rock, a sandstone cliff at a desert watering place on which are carved hundreds of inscriptions, including those of early Spanish explorers and early American immigrants.
Notes: Guided tours, camping; elevation 7,218 feet.
Address: Ramah, N.M. 87321.

Pecos National Monument
Ruins of strategically located Indian town at gateway between the Great Plains and Rio Grande Valley that was visited by Coronado in 1541; also remains of several Spanish mission churches.
Notes: Guided tours; elevation 7,000 feet.
Address: Drawer 11, Pecos, N.M. 87552.

UTAH

Arches National Park (Chapter 8)
Remarkable products of erosion in the heart of the red-rock country; some ninety arches as well as spires, pinnacles, and balanced rocks.
Notes: Guided tours, camping, hiking; lodging and food near park; elevation 4,085–5,650 feet.
Address: c/o Canyonlands National Park, Post Office Building, Moab, Utah 84532.

Bryce Canyon National Park
Horseshoe-shaped amphitheater along the edge of Paunsaugunt Plateau, containing perhaps the most colorful and unusual erosional forms in the world.
Notes: Guided tours, camping, hiking, horseback riding; lodging and food in park; elevation 7,586–9,105 feet.

Address: Bryce Canyon, Utah 84717.

Canyonlands National Park (Chapter 11)
High mesas offering thrilling views, canyons, great arches of striking
beauty, pinnacles, and countless other rock forms.
Notes: Camping, hiking, boating; elevation 3,600–7,000 feet.
Address: Post Office Building, Moab, Utah 84532.

Capitol Reef National Park (Chapter 12)
A great sandstone cliff, cut by narrow canyons and carved into fan-
tastic domes, towers, and spires, rising abruptly above the desert
floor.
Notes: Guided tours, camping, hiking, fishing; lodging and food near
park; elevation 5,300 feet.
Address: Torrey, Utah 84775.

Cedar Breaks National Monument
Gigantic natural amphitheater eroded into the variegated Pink Cliffs;
mountain meadows, aspen, and other plants of the high country.
Closed in winter.
Notes: Guided tours, camping, hiking; lodging and food in park;
elevation 10,400 feet.
Address: c/o Zion National Park, Springdale, Utah 84767.

Glen Canyon Recreation Area
Lake Powell, formed by Glen Canyon Dam, will be 186 miles long
when filled, with 1,800 miles of shore line, including colorful fiord-
like side canyons.
Notes: Camping, hiking, hunting, swimming, boating, fishing, other
water sports; lodging and food in park; elevation 3,000–5,000 feet.
Address: Box 1507, Page, Ariz. 86040.

Natural Bridges National Monument
Three large natural bridges carved from sandstone; the highest, 220
feet above the stream bed, has a span of 261 feet. Isolated area.
Notes: Camping, hiking; elevation 6,000 feet.
Address: c/o Canyonlands National Park, Post Office Building,
Moab, Utah 84532.

Rainbow Bridge National Monument
Greatest of known natural bridges; a symmetrical arch of salmon-
pink sandstone rising 309 feet above bottom of gorge.
Notes: Hiking.

Address: c/o Glen Canyon Recreation Area, Box 1507, Page, Ariz. 86040.

Zion National Park (Chapter 16)
Multicolored Zion Canyon, with its high sheer walls, equally color-ful finger canyons—great heights, great distances. Awesome.
Notes: Guided tours, camping, hiking, horseback riding, swimming, fishing; lodging and food in park; elevation 4,400–7,800 feet.
Address: Springdale, Utah 84767.

The foregoing list includes only national parks and monuments under the administration of the National Park Service. There are

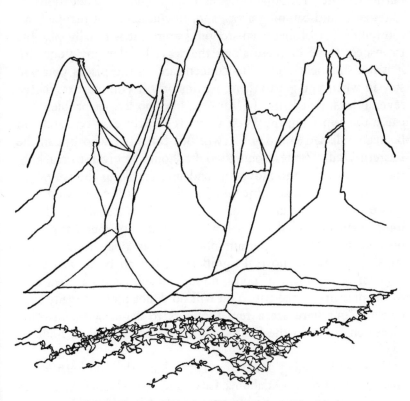

The Three Patriarchs (Zion National Park)

many other places that should also be considered in your plans. First of all, there are the Indian reservations (see Chapter 17). There are also the national forests, administered by the U.S. Department of Agriculture. Here you will find campgrounds in cool, wooded settings and abundant bird and animal life. Most of the state maps published by gasoline companies show the locations of the national forests and the camping areas in them. It is difficult to plan such camping in advance, but if you allow yourself enough time you will find opportunities to go into some of the forests along your route for an overnight stop or simply a refreshing lunchtime picnic.

In addition to all of these, there are the state parks, including particularly Dead Horse Point, Utah, which is described in detail in Chapter 13. Again the state maps show the locations of state parks and camping areas, and, if you have not mapped out too long a stretch between stopping points, it is usually possible to inspect some of these along the way. In planning your trip it is not sufficient merely to concentrate on the places you will stay in when you get to them, particularly if you must travel for several days. Residents of California have no serious problem because the trip from the West Coast is a fairly easy one and can be accomplished in a day or two. But for those who live in the Eastern United States, some thought should be given to reaching the Southwest with enjoyment and interest along the way.

Obviously the main objective in driving to the Southwest is to arrive there safely and in one piece. But several days, all day long, spent crammed into a hot vehicle are not much fun with no diversions. It is important not to fritter away time on side trips which are of no real significance, but an occasional short stop for refreshment of body, mind, and spirit adds a great deal to the pleasure of the trip. You will no doubt pick up many suggestions, but here are a few thoughts to begin with on some places en route to the Southwest which are worth an hour or two.

For those coming from the East along the southern route through St. Louis, Oklahoma City, and Amarillo, Texas, there is a delightful detour off Interstate 44 to Claremore, Oklahoma. This is the Will Rogers Memorial, a museum built by the State

of Oklahoma three years after Rogers's tragic death in 1935. On
display are personal effects and memorabilia from all over the
world, including Rogers's fascinating collection of saddles. There
is also a group of dioramas tracing his life. One poignant exhibit
includes the twisted portable typewriter on which he was writing a column when the plane in which he and Wiley Post were
flying crashed in Alaska. In the foyer, near a bronze statue by
Jo Davidson, is a speaker which, at the push of a button, affords
members of a newer generation the chance to hear short recordings of some of Will Rogers's monologues. Although much of
the humor is topical, the style and delivery are still fresh, and
appreciative laughter echoes delightfully in the chamber.

Oklahoma City is the home of the National Cowboy Hall of
Fame, with its art gallery featuring works by Russell and Remington, its collection of American sculpture, its Museum of
Western History, and the Rodeo Hall of Fame. An eye-popping
assemblage.

Those who come by way of Kansas City may drive through
Colorado Springs, which provides an opportunity to visit the
U.S. Air Force Academy. Among the worthwhile things to see
here are the exceptionally good orientation film shown at the
visitors' center; the remarkable chapel, whose interior exceeds
its dazzling exterior in beauty of design; and the comings and
goings of the cadets across the Cadet Area, where these newest
arrivals are required to run from place to place along the walks
and must cut their corners square, following the straight lines of
the walks. Diagonal short cuts or even a curve around the bend
are taboo. If you are particularly fortunate, you may run into
a falconer exercising one of the Academy's mascots.

Along the northern route—through Des Moines, Iowa; Omaha,
Nebraska; and Cheyenne, Wyoming—there are at least three
unusual side trips which are well worth stopping for. At Grand
Island, Nebraska, off Interstate 80, is the Stuhr Museum, a small,
sparkling white gem set in the midst of the great flat plain.
Edward Durell Stone designed the main building. Inside, the
entrance leads to a miniature central court with goldfish pools
and cool green plantings. From this court, two graceful staircases
curve up to the exhibit areas above. Here are handsome displays

reflecting the frontier life of Nebraska's rural areas and small towns in the late nineteenth century, among the best exhibits of Americana to be seen anywhere in the country. Not far from the main museum building is an outdoor museum, brought together from various parts of Nebraska, consisting of a whole village of structures reflecting the life of the period—church, post office, stores, houses—most of which can be explored inside as well as out. The easy pace and openness of the Stuhr Museum are special added attractions for those used to visiting museums in crowded urban centers.

At North Platte, Nebraska, if you find yourself there in August, there are regular evening performances during that month of "Buffalo Bill's Wild West and Congress of Rough Riders of the World." The performers do a creditable job of duplicating the program which made the former Indian scout famous worldwide. The show is held on grounds which were once a part of the great showman's own ranch and includes a herd of buffaloes, Indian dances, a noisy stagecoach attack, trick lariat roping, and plenty of daredevil horseback riding. The finale—as all of the performers in the show thunder on horseback full circle around the arena at breakneck speed, led at a wide-open gallop by an American Indian in splendid regalia mounted on a white horse and holding aloft the American flag which streams out behind him, with a background of sky rockets bursting overhead—is likely to choke up even the most hardbitten and sophisticated.

At Cheyenne, Wyoming, visitors are permitted to tour the Wyoming Hereford Ranch. This ranch, which covers 60,000 acres, has a herd of 2,500 registered Herefords, generating breeding stock for many of the cattle raisers of the West. Particularly for city dwellers, a visit to the ranch is a good low-key way to see another part of the American scene at first hand. The top breeding and show animals, when they are at the ranch, are particularly impressive.

Enjoying the Southwest is the principal purpose of your visit, but careful planning of the trip out and back will add happy and interesting dimensions to the whole expedition.

8
Arches National Park (Utah)

Cowboys say that it is foolhardy to build a pine board fence in the desert. "The wind will blow through the knotholes and wear the boards out." Desert winds blowing through small holes in the sandstone have created almost ninety arches of stone at Arches National Park—many of them so striking that they defy description.

A 300-foot layer of red sandstone, called by geologists the Entrada sandstone bed, was laid down in this area about 150 million years ago. Indications are that the sand was part of a huge coastal desert which was later submerged and covered over by new layers, all of which became hardened into rock. Later the rock area was raised up to an elevation of about 5,000 feet, cracking in the process. A series of cracks ten to twenty feet apart fractured the Entrada sandstone bed, and, as the upper layers weathered away, water entered the cracks, weakening the sandstone, loosening the sand, and permitting wind and water to continue the erosion process, resulting in the unusual geological formations which stand today.

Arches National Park, one of the lesser-known park areas open to the public, was established in 1929 and covers 137 square miles. It was not until 1937 that visitors were first able to enter

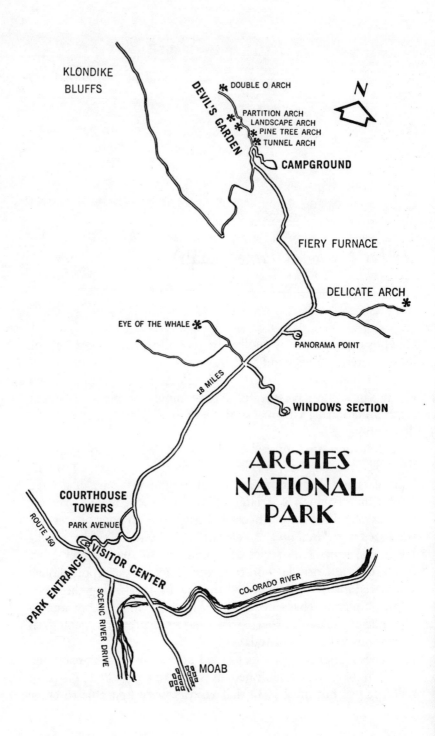

KLONDIKE BLUFFS

DEVIL'S GARDEN

N

* DOUBLE O ARCH

PARTITION ARCH
LANDSCAPE ARCH
* PINE TREE ARCH
* TUNNEL ARCH

CAMPGROUND

FIERY FURNACE

DELICATE ARCH *

EYE OF THE WHALE *

PANORAMA POINT

18 MILES

WINDOWS SECTION

ARCHES
NATIONAL
PARK

COURTHOUSE
TOWERS

PARK AVENUE

ROUTE 160

VISITOR CENTER

PARK ENTRANCE

SCENIC RIVER DRIVE

COLORADO RIVER

MOAB

the park area by road. Now an excellent paved road runs through the center of the park, making access quite easy.

There are four principal stone masses along the 18-mile road through the park area. The first of these is located just above the entrance and visitors' center. After a fairly steep climb, one comes upon a towering group of stone shapes known as Courthouse Towers. There is a foot trail through the center of this group which is reasonably easy to walk. One member of the party can drive farther on along the road to pick up the hikers as they emerge on the other side. The hiking path has been dubbed Park Avenue. The rock forms in the Courthouse Towers area trigger the imagination easily. The huge shapes are reminiscent of ancient classical architecture. If one were to design the city of the gods on Mount Olympus, it might look something like the Courthouse Towers in scale and dramatic impact.

The second principal area, 9 miles from the entrance, is the Windows section. A 3-mile side road leads into this area and provides handsome views not only of rock masses pierced by arches but also of a number of freestanding groups which have the appearance of human figures and could easily provide inspiration for the British sculptor Henry Moore.

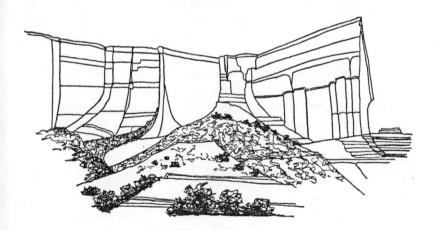

Arches National Park

A few miles farther on is the third area, reached by a short unpaved side road, which leads to a view of Delicate Arch, with a foot trail of 1½ miles up to the arch for the hardy. Delicate Arch is one of the most celebrated sights in the park.

The fourth principal area of rock formations in Arches National Park is Devil's Garden, at the end of the 18-mile drive. Here are located sixty-four of the known arches, extending along a continuous sandstone ridge. The 2-mile foot trail through the Devil's Garden provides good views of Tunnel Arch, Pine Tree Arch, Landscape Arch, Partition Arch, and Double O Arch.

The campground at Arches is unusually attractive. The camp spaces are well separated so that most sites have an unobstructed view, taking in a wide sweep of the surrounding natural beauty. Sunrise is particularly dramatic, as the sun's rays strike the tops of the red sandstone shapes which rise on the periphery of the camping area.

There are nightly campfire programs for visitors. Sometimes, if you are lucky, the park ranger who conducts the talk will turn out to be a superb natural storyteller who can hold a group of campers spellbound for an hour with stories about camping, western outlaws, or anything else that comes to mind.

Arches National Park deserves a two-day visit in itself, but there are also some connecting benefits which are worth stopping for. The park is located 5 miles northwest of the small city of Moab, which was first settled by Mormons in 1855. Forty-one men left Salt Lake City in the spring of that year with fifteen wagons, thirteen horses, sixty-five oxen, sixteen cows, two bulls, one calf, two pigs, twelve chickens, four dogs, and a supply of flour, wheat, oats, corn, potatoes, and peas, plus five plows, twenty-two axes and other tools. By midsummer the men had planted crops and built a stone fort. In late September the Indians suddenly initiated a series of attacks, killing three Mormons and setting fire to haystacks and fences. The men abandoned the fort the following morning. When later settlers attempted to occupy the area after twenty years had passed, they too had problems with Indian attacks. In the end, things settled down and a peaceful community took root. Moab itself is a friendly town, and there are many interesting things to see and do in the surrounding countryside. A visit to the Moab Chamber of Commerce can produce valuable advice on places to visit.

Among the rewarding side trips is a drive along the Colorado River, starting from the entrance to Arches National Park (one can unhitch a trailer and leave it in the parking lot before starting). A good paved road runs north and south along the river's edge, affording dramatic views of the cliffs which the river has created. Following the road south from the Arches entrance, it is approximately 16 miles to a large potash mine and the end of the paved surface, and along the route one may see Indian markings and dinosaur tracks. In a remote part of this area is a petroglyph, 42 inches wide and 14 inches high, of what is believed to be a mastodon with an upturned trunk. Since it is also believed that mastodons became extinct 30,000 years ago, there is a nice archaeological riddle as to whether the mastodon survived later or whether man occupied this area earlier than other evidences indicate.

The unique feature of Arches National Park is its rock formations and groupings which stir the imagination. Handsome and unusual scenic beauty, combined with good camping facilities and the advantages of interesting side trips, make a visit well worthwhile.

Arches National Park

9
Bandelier National Monument (New Mexico)

It would be hard to find a more satisfying archaeological experience than a visit to Bandelier National Monument. Located 46 miles west of Santa Fe, New Mexico (north from Santa Fe on U.S. 285 to Pojoaque, then west on State 4), Bandelier represents the historical bridge in the transition of the earliest Indian inhabitants from their original cliff dwellings in Mesa Verde and adjoining areas to the modern pueblo Indians of today. The monument was named in honor of a Swiss-American scholar who lived in one of the ruins here during the 1880's while conducting the first scientific studies of the area and its people.

The principal archaeological ruins at Bandelier are located in a canyon which can be reached by a good paved road. The ruins are easily explored on foot, with plenty of opportunity to examine and reflect. The setting is intriguing both because of its natural beauty and its unusual geological qualities. The excavations have been handled with restraint and good taste, so that one can still enjoy a sense of the excitement of discovery.

Bandelier is located on the Pajarito Plateau at the foot of the Jemez Mountains. The mountains form the east rim of a great ancient volcano—long extinct—which showered the ash that created the plateau. This volcanic material which comprises the

154

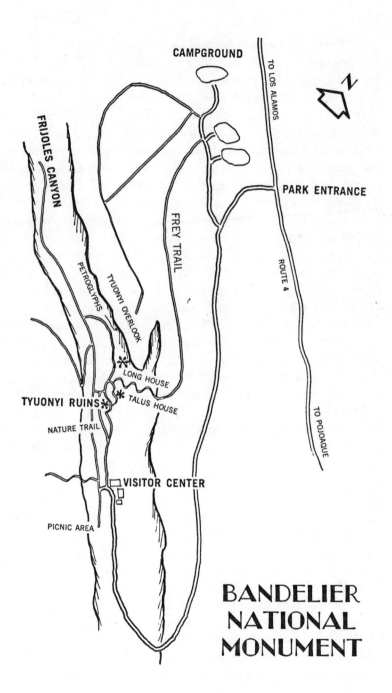

CAMPGROUND

TO LOS ALAMOS

PARK ENTRANCE

FRIJOLES CANYON

FREY TRAIL

ROUTE 4

PETROGLYPHS

TYUONYI OVERLOOK

LONG HOUSE

TYUONYI RUINS

TALUS HOUSE

TO POJOAQUE

NATURE TRAIL

VISITOR CENTER

PICNIC AREA

N

BANDELIER NATIONAL MONUMENT

present-day plateau was welded together as it eroded, eventually forming a soft, easily carved rock called "tuff." The Pajarito Plateau is regarded as one of the outstanding examples of tuff formations in the world.

It is the remarkable composition of the volcanic tuff which made possible the unique features of the Bandelier ruins, which include the remains not only of extensive pueblo-style masonry structures but also of rooms dug out of the face of the tuff cliff, as well as a combination of these two types of dwellings. This combination, called a talus house, made use of the cliff for a back wall, usually with a cave room in it and with masonry walls extending out from it. The roof beams of these talus houses were held in place, on the cliff end, by small holes which can be seen today in evenly spaced rows above many of the cave rooms. Often, a family would start out with a cave room and then, as more space was needed, build extensions out from it.

The early residents of Bandelier are believed to have numbered as many as 1,500 to 2,000 at one time. They came to the area in about A.D. 1280, at a time when the areas to the west were in the process of abandonment because of the great drought. The principal attraction was the stream which flowed—and still flows —through the canyon, guaranteeing greater fertility for agriculture than reliance on erratic rainfalls elsewhere. The Indian farmers occupied the area for approximately three centuries and then moved on at about the time the Spanish first arrived in the Southwest. Every indication is that the present Indian inhabitants of the pueblos along the Rio Grande River, just a few miles away, are descendants of the Indian inhabitants of Bandelier who moved on to the present sites 300 years ago.

The entire area around the plateau and up the eastern slope of the Jemez Mountains was apparently thickly settled at one time. Bandelier National Monument covers more than 46 square miles of this area, including countless unexcavated ruins, but its principal archaeological ruins are located in Frijoles Canyon. The similarities between the ruins excavated at Bandelier and present-day pueblo communities are striking and add to the excitement of exploring the monument. Here are community structures containing as many as five or six hundred rooms, together with the communal kiva used then, and still today, for ceremonial and meeting purposes.

In the wooded canyon which is the center of Bandelier National Monument are ruins of structures which contained, in their prime, more than a thousand rooms, together with the excavated remains of the largest kiva found anywhere in the area. The most impressive ruin is Tyuonyi, located prominently in the center of the canyon a short distance from the present visitor center. Although only portions of the ground floor walls remain, it is possible to count more than 250 rooms on this level alone. These ruins make a striking pattern when viewed from above, for they are arranged in concentric rows around a central plaza. In the widest section, the rooms are eight deep; in the narrowest, four deep. The absence of fireplaces and ventilation—affording protection against rodents and vermin—indicates that many of these ground-floor rooms were used to store food supplies over the winter.

Undoubtedly Tyuonyi was designed to provide a kind of fortress for defense against surprise attack. There is a single

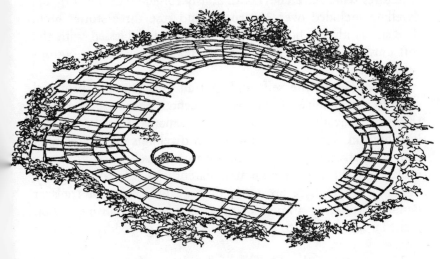

Ruins of Tyuonyi (Bandelier National Monument)

entrance door into the central plaza, and apparently the structure included two upper stories, with rooms which had no windows or doors but only a hole in the roof. Entrance to these rooms was gained by ladders. Drawing up the ladders and blocking the passageways provided a quick means of defense against attack.

One of the striking features of the rooms themselves is their small size, although they apparently accommodated many residents—this being made possible by the absence of furniture. The ingenious dating method used by archaeologists in the Southwest based on the tree rings in ceiling beams (described in Chapter 3 and covered by an excellent display in the museum at Mesa Verde) indicates that Tyuonyi was built over a span of several decades before and after the year 1400.

Some of Bandelier's unique talus houses, which ring the canyon walls and which apparently were built to handle overflow population, can be seen directly above Tyuonyi. A section of this area has been reconstructed by the Museum of New Mexico to show a typical talus house. Of special interest is a small cave kiva whose walls are covered with decorations representing dancing figures and a feathered serpent. Farther up the canyon is a ruin called Long House, a combination of cave rooms and masonry structures which stretches continuously for 800 feet. The original dwelling included over 300 rooms and rose three stories high. The site is idyllic, being slightly elevated and blessed with the soft music of running water and the coolness of nearby cottonwood trees.

In addition to the self-guiding trail covering the principal ruins in the vicinity of the visitors' center, there are also trails to other excavations, including the Ceremonial Cave, a restored kiva built in conjunction with several dwellings on a ledge high above the stream and protected by a great arch of overhanging rock, and a shrine of stone lions apparently used for offerings by hunters. In all, there are more than 60 miles of foot trails at Bandelier, offering a range of opportunities from an impression picked up in an hour to a more studied view gained by a two- or three-day visit.

The campground, at the top of the canyon, is spacious, attractive, and cool. There is also an older lodge facility next to the visitors' center, as well as a shop offering some remarkably nice examples of Indian arts and crafts.

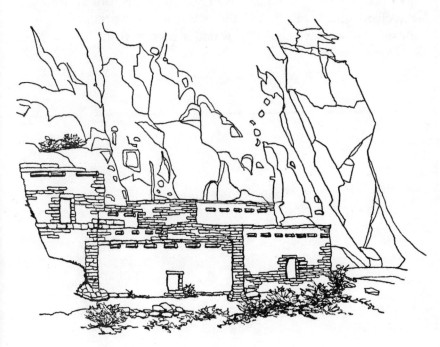

Talus House (Bandelier National Monument)

The surrounding country holds many pleasures. The city of Santa Fe contains a number of handsome old structures, although the city itself has become somewhat spoiled by an overemphasis on tourism. Along the Rio Grande River are a number of modern Indian pueblos, each of which has a special flavor and interest of its own. Best known of these is Taos Pueblo, about 75 miles to the north. Although it too has become overrun with tourists, the basic features of the pueblo construction and design are striking and make it well worth an hour's visit if one's route goes in that direction.

A landmark of a different sort is the community of Los Alamos, headquarters of the United States Atomic Energy Commission. A drive through this clinically forbidding laboratory area presents stark contrasts to the surrounding natural beauty, the charm and fascination of the pueblos, and the reminders, on all sides, of ancient civilizations and a simpler past.

10
Canyon de Chelly
National Monumeut (Arizona)

After their Long Walk in 1864, 8,000 Navajo Indians lived huddled together in an early version of a concentration camp near Fort Sumner, New Mexico. In 1868 a government peace commission headed by General William T. Sherman entered into negotiations with the Navajos which resulted in the peace treaty that established the Navajo reservation. During the course of the negotiations, the spokesman for the Navajos was Chief Barboncito, who explained the plight of his people and asked that they be allowed to return to the home of their forefathers, of which Canyon de Chelly was the center. Chief Barboncito predicted that if his people could return to Canyon de Chelly and its surrounding countryside, their troubles would be over and they would not trouble others.

"After we get back to our country it will brighten up again and the Navajos will be as happy as the land, black clouds will rise, and there will be plenty of rain. Corn will grow in abundance, and everything look happy."

The place to which Chief Barboncito referred so poetically is still there, and it does look happy. Canyon de Chelly is one of the crown jewels of the Southwest. Its scenery is quietly

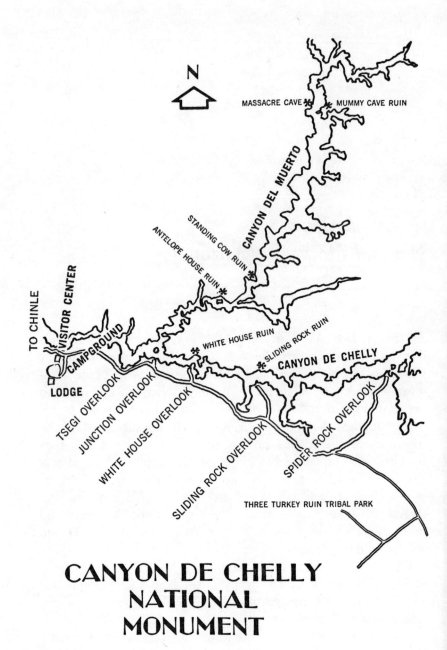

N

MASSACRE CAVE ✳   ✳ MUMMY CAVE RUIN

CANYON DEL MUERTO

STANDING COW RUIN

ANTELOPE HOUSE RUIN ✳

TO CHINLE

VISITOR CENTER

CAMPGROUND

LODGE

WHITE HOUSE RUIN   SLIDING ROCK RUIN

CANYON DE CHELLY

TSEGI OVERLOOK

JUNCTION OVERLOOK

WHITE HOUSE OVERLOOK

SLIDING ROCK OVERLOOK

SPIDER ROCK OVERLOOK

THREE TURKEY RUIN TRIBAL PARK

CANYON DE CHELLY
NATIONAL
MONUMENT

beautiful, its archaeological treasures are astonishing, and it provides to this day a vibrant life stream for 500 Navajos who still farm on the canyon floor. Canyon de Chelly is in human scale. Its walls are made of red sandstone whose hue varies with the different times and moods of the day. The shadows on the sculptured faces of the cliffs and on the cottonwood trees—direct complementary color to the red of the cliffs—provide fresh patterns in every direction. As one stands on the rim of the canyon looking down, one can see the hogans of the Indians, their fields of corn, the tiny figures of horses and goats, and the tracks of animals and vehicles. Here is a spirit of vitality which carries on an ancient tradition of life in a setting which is over 200 million years old.

During the Permian Period, about 230 million years ago, the inland seas which covered much of North America disappeared as the earth's crust buckled and the land mass created high mountains which blocked the movement of the moisture-laden prevailing winds, resulting in a parched desert where plant and animal life could not survive. Dry winds took over and created massive sand dunes, some of them hundreds of feet deep.

Canyon de Chelly is one of those sand dunes, later converted to rock under the pressure of subsequent layers of conglomerates and other materials which in time weathered away. The upper layers included the formations in which petrified forests and dinosaur tracks have been found, but at Canyon de Chelly all of these other formations have disappeared and only the earlier sandstone remains.

Fifty million years ago another upheaval of the earth's surface forced the rise in the land, which permitted streams flowing down from nearby mountains to cut into the sandstone and create canyons. The uplift was at an angle, with the result that Canyon de Chelly slopes from a depth of only a few feet at its western end to a thousand feet on the east, adding to its interest and diversity.

Over the course of years, freezing water, tree roots, and other eroding elements have caused the walls of the canyon to be cut with myriad facets which respond to sunlight and shadow in a

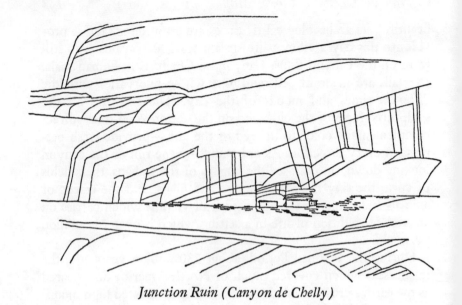

Junction Ruin (Canyon de Chelly)

dramatic variety of ways. This variety is heightened by the streaking of many of the rock faces, as rain and ground water have dissolved manganese and iron oxides in the sandstone and brought them to the surface where they have hardened. Wind-blown sand has polished these surface encrustations, giving sections of the canyon walls a look of perpetual wetness.

Canyon de Chelly is rich in archaeological sites, covering a period of occupancy over some two thousand years. Two separate groups of early inhabitants made their way there. The first were the Anasazi, the people who occupied the plateau area of the Southwest starting about A.D. 200. These "ancient ones" passed through various stages of development, reaching a fairly high state of civilization in the thirteenth century, when, as in other areas of the Southwest, they abandoned their established homes on a wholesale basis, apparently because of extensive drought. Archaeological discoveries covering all stages of the evolution of the Anasazi have been found in Canyon de Chelly. Invaluable evidence of occupation during the Basketmaker Period was found in Mummy Cave in Canyon del Muerto, the northern branch of the monument. One researcher discovered among the debris a wooden pole which had been cut in the year 348. Recesses in the canyon walls contain the ruins of many structures built during subsequent centuries.

The largest and best preserved of the ruins in the monument is the White House, which was occupied between A.D. 1050 and 1300, during the great Pueblo Period. It is a combination of buildings on the canyon floor and in a cavity of the canyon wall just above. Apparently the lower structures once rose to a height of four or five stories, with ladders extending to the large upper building. The remains of four kivas have been excavated in the lower site.

The second group of people to become inhabitants of Canyon de Chelly were the forebears of today's Navajo Indians. This second group called themselves Dineh, the People, and after many years of wandering they came to settle down in and around Canyon de Chelly. They came slowly, and by degrees, but by the end of the eighteenth century were well established here. Along the way, they had picked up customs and skills from other Indian tribes, including the agricultural and wool-raising and weaving knowledge of the Pueblo peoples—whose ancestors were the Anasazi—and thus the Navajos brought to Canyon de Chelly not only their own vitality and broadly based culture but returned as well skills which had left there centuries before.

A grim landmark of this later period of history exists at the eastern end of Canyon del Muerto, at a spot now known as Massacre Cave. Here, in the year 1805, Navajo Indians took shelter on a high ledge to ward off a troop of Spanish soldiers who had come into their stronghold. The ledge had proved invincible in combat with other Indians, but the Spaniards sent soldiers armed with muskets to the canyon rim, where they could take deadly aim. The Spanish lieutenant in charge of the foray reported killing 115 Navajos and taking 33 prisoners. He said that 90 of those killed were warriors and proved it by sending their ears to the Spanish governor in Santa Fe. The Spaniards lost one man.

The Spanish attack at Massacre Cave was the result of treachery by a young Navajo who had been refused the hand of a girl belonging to one of the clans. In his anger, the disappointed youth took his revenge by guiding the Spaniards into the canyon.

Present-day visitors have many exiting opportunities to see and enjoy Canyon de Chelly. There is a rim drive, which can be covered by automobile in a couple of hours, and which leads to five overlooks of the canyon at its different depths: Tsegi, Junction, White House, Sliding Rock, and Spider Rock. Spider Rock is a sandstone spire which soars 800 feet from the canyon

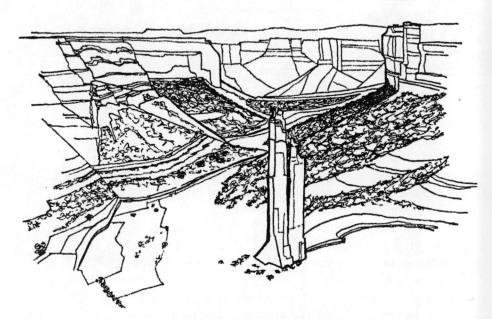

Spider Rock (Canyon de Chelly)

floor. Viewed from an overlook itself 1,000 feet high, it is one of the most dramatic sights in the Southwest. The principal difference between the vistas in Canyon de Chelly and more publicized sights, such as those in Grand Canyon and Bryce Canyon, is that the scale of Canyon de Chelly is enough smaller that human beings can feel that they are part of what they are seeing.

Visitors are not permitted to walk into the canyon at any point, with the exception of a foot trail which leads down the cliff at the White House overlook to allow a close examination of the ruins of this remarkable pueblo cliff dwelling. There is also an early morning nature walk, led by a park ranger, which takes about two hours and gives visitors a chance to explore the lower end of the canyon on foot.

The most exciting way to see Canyon de Chelly is on horseback. A corral is maintained at the monument where horses can be hired for group trips under the leadership of an experienced guide. The guide often turns out to be a Navajo boy. The experience has none of the commercialism which marks many of the horseback rides in the more popular park areas. A three-hour ride along the canyon floor, with its patterns of shadows and water ripple marks and blowing grasses—watching the changing sunlight and shadow on the red sandstone cliffs which rise on all sides; riding past the flocks of sheep and goats, the bands of semi-wild horses, and the Navajo farms—is an experience that one will not soon forget.

Arrangements can also be made to tour the canyon in vehicles with four-wheel drive which are operated by Thunderbird Lodge, a concession located in the monument area. These tours are half day or full day, depending on how much of the canyon one wishes to see. The full day tour covers the principal portions of both branches of the canyon—Canyon de Chelly and also Canyon del Muerto.

The campground at Canyon de Chelly is located in a grove of cottonwood trees, and although it is at times more crowded than those of some other national monuments it is still extremely pleasant, and the shade from the trees is most welcome during the hot part of the day. There are nightly campfire talks, including presentations by National Park Service employees who are Navajo Indians. The Thunderbird Lodge operates a cafeteria which is open to all visitors, so that campers who are so inclined can have the variety of a meal out once in a while.

The visitors' center at Canyon de Chelly is outstanding. The exhibits themselves are well executed, and if you are lucky there will be two Navajo women on the scene, quietly demonstrating their skills, one weaving a rug or belt and the other making a basket, giving you an opportunity to observe these operations first-hand. There is also an excellent selection of books for sale at the desk.

In the adjoining city of Chinle, one can visit the Canyon de Chelly Trading Post and see a modern-day version of this venerable institution in operation. The trading post provides a unique banking facility. An Indian farmer can pledge a piece of silver and turquoise jewelry, a fine woven rug, or other article of value to obtain credit for the purchase of food and clothing during the period between crops, and then redeem his articles when he has cash in hand. No interest is charged for any period up to six months. In Chinle also is a branch store of the Navajo Arts and Crafts Guild, which sells the very best of the Navajo jewelry and rugs and has the advantage of fixed prices for those who do not like the haggling which is expected in most of the trading posts and other places where such items are sold.

For those who are seeking the quiet charms and beauties of the Southwest and a glimpse of its Indian heritage, past and present, Canyon de Chelly National Monument should head the list. One should plan to spend three or four days here to savor fully its pleasures.

The canyon's chief protection against being overwhelmed by tourists is its relative inaccessibility, for a trip requires traveling a good many miles into the heart of the Navajo reservation. The park entrance is on the east side of Chinle, which is off State 63 in the northeastern corner of Arizona.

11
Canyonlands National Park (Utah)

In 1836 a guide named Denis Julien attained an immortality of sorts by carving his name in the rock wall near the place where the Green River and the Colorado River come together in southeastern Utah. Shortly thereafter Julien disappeared from sight after heading into the rapids in Cataract Canyon, where he presumably drowned. Julien was the first white man known to have traveled through the magnificent country which now constitutes Canyonlands National Park. Not many people have followed him.

The next known explorer was Captain John N. Macomb, who passed that way in 1859, viewed the confluence of the rivers from the canyon rim, and reported in disgust, "I cannot conceive of a more worthless and impractical region."

Ten years later Major John Wesley Powell, the one-armed Civil War veteran who headed a team of geologists and geographers on a mission to explore and map the Colorado River area, sounded a somewhat more optimistic note when he reached the point where the Green and Colorado rivers meet. The major recorded the discovery of "ten thousand strangely carved forms . . . and beyond them mountains blending with the clouds."

After that, scant attention was paid to this forbidding area,

and few people ventured into it—except for an occasional runaway outlaw—until 1952, when the frenzy of the post-World
War II uranium boom sent prospectors in four-wheel-drive Jeeps
careering into all corners of Utah looking for sites that would

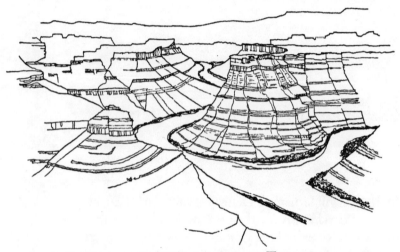

Confluence of the Green and Colorado Rivers
(Canyonlands National Park)

make them millionaires overnight. None were found in Canyonlands itself, but word of its beauty trickled back. Finally, in 1964,
Congress designated the huge area of 257,640 acres surrounding
the juncture of the two rivers as a national park.

Even today, few people know this wonderful land of spectacular rock masses, plunging canyons, and sharp contrasts. Only a
fraction of the park is accessible by automobile, and all indications are that the area will remain wild and undeveloped.

Canyonlands National Park lies to the northeast of the Glen
Canyon National Recreation Area, that once-glorious string of
canyons which have now been filled up with a muddy lake behind Glen Canyon Dam. Canyonlands begins as a 2,000-foot-
deep canyon, just below Dead Horse Point. The ravine opens
up below that point into a wide valley of rock forms which have

been eroded and carved into numberless shapes and sizes. The rock itself averages 150 million years old, younger than the deeper strata of the Grand Canyon to the south. The oldest rocks to be found in Canyonlands today date from the Carboniferous Period, some 300 million years ago, when many of the rich eastern coal beds were being created.

The park is a veritable city of pinnacles, monuments, and arches. The variation in the deposit layers which make up these forms, and their consequent differences in hardness from top to bottom, helps to explain their variety in shape and size. The arches were created when the soft sandstone of the bottom layer weathered away more quickly than the harder stone at the top.

A visitor to Canyonlands National Park is bound to feel a sense of excitement and adventure as he approaches the area. The route leading in, which starts 15 miles north of Monticello, Utah, is a 30-mile-long paved road which heads west, traveling through arid desert country which gradually changes to rougher terrain until its final conversion to the red standstone cliffs and monuments. Approximately midway along the road is a small state park at Indian Creek, where, in a setting of cottonwood trees, underneath a protective overhanging ledge, there is a 20-foot-high darkened stone surface on which some ancient Indian visitors carved their petroglyphs and drawings. This intriguing primitive mural is known as Newspaper Rock.

After Indian Creek, the road into the Needles District of Canyonlands National Park begins to go through grander scenery, with bold cliffs running parallel to the road for many miles, the distance between them widening as the road nears its end. Curiously, the quality of the paved road improves at this point, and travel is extremely easy right up to the ranger station just inside the park boundary. The ranger station is nothing more than a metal trailer, with an air conditioner usually operating full blast. The rangers on duty seem glad to have visitors and are most helpful with information and good advice.

The campground, in an area called Squaw Flat, 2 miles beyond the ranger station, is perhaps the nicest campground in the South-

CANYONLANDS NATIONAL PARK

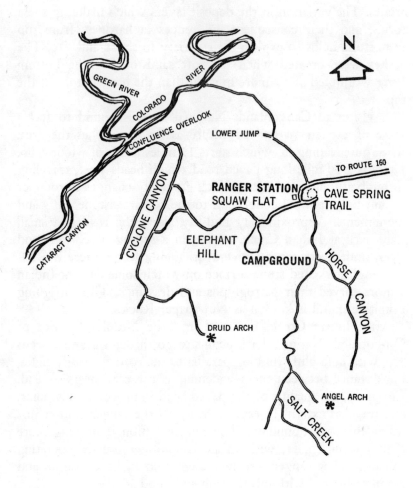

west. The camp spaces are located well apart from each other and nestled into a rock formation which seems to have been set there by nature just for the purpose. In contrast to the hard lines of commercial campgrounds, the good taste, good judgment, and sensitivity shown in locating the campsites at Squaw Flat contribute to a lovely and peaceful stay. The sanitary facilities are somewhat primitive for those who are used to modern fixtures: fiberglass privies. But in the setting and spirit of this untamed area, they are right, and if one discreetly slips a foot in the door, the pleasures of contemplating the desert while paying a visit would have the full approval of Chic Sale. The campsites are generously shaded by juniper trees which, when laden with pungent berries in midsummer, scent the air delightfully.

There are a number of trails in the Canyonlands area, but none made for the family car. A four-wheel-drive vehicle can be driven on some; for the rest, one must go on foot. A commercial facility located just outside the entrance to the park advertises guided tours by four-wheel-drive vehicle into some of the areas inaccessible by standard automobile.

There is an especially enjoyable short foot trail, located approximately ¾ mile from the ranger station, the starting point of which is easily reached by automobile. This is the Cave Spring Environmental Trail, which wanders in and around a small but interesting rocky area for approximately half a mile. On this trail, one passes under a ledge created by erosion where one can see badger holes, anthills, and pack rat nests, some going back hundreds and possibly thousands of years. On the surface of the ledge, above, one is likely to see a ground squirrel or rock squirrel and possibly several different kinds of small lizards. The trail leads to the cave for which it is named, actually a huge hollowed-out space under another large rock ledge. At the back of the cave is the spring, a fine continual trickle of clear water. The roof of the cave is blackened by smoke, and on the walls may be seen pictograph paintings giving clear evidence that Anasazi Indian families once lived here. Farther on, under still another ledge, there is a more modern line camp set up by cowboys as a base of operations while they were tending the herds that grazed the surrounding countryside starting in the 1890's. The cattle were moved on after they had finally destroyed most of the desert grass. Half-empty containers of provisions, old cornflake boxes, coffee tins, and other indicia of recent occupation still remain in the line camp cave, giving pointed emphasis to the spread of history which is encompassed by this short walk.

Because of its relative inaccessibility, Canyonlands National Park is lightly visited. Because it is still essentially a desert wilderness, the impact on those who do manage to go there is correspondingly great. Here in fact is an unspoiled wilderness area which one can explore today with something of the wonder and excitement surely felt by Major Powell and other daring adventurers of years gone by. Here one is completely out of touch with modern civilization. Here one still stands in awe of the natural miracles of earth and sky.

12
Capitol Reef National Park (Utah)

When the antipolygamy laws were passed in 1886, the Mormon families who had settled in the small community of Fruita, Utah, searched for a possible hideout in the event that law enforcement officers came looking for polygamists in their area. They selected a narrow and fractured canyon, with a maze of side canyons, as an ideal place in which to avoid pursuit. Thereafter it was nick-named Cohabitation Canyon. The name has stuck, in shortened form, and the place is still called Cohab Canyon in honor of this brief period in history.

Cohab Canyon is one of many intriguing formations in Capitol Reef National Park. Located in the south-central section of Utah, the park is reached over State 24 after a good many miles of driving. The park was quite isolated until recently, as the eastern leg of this road was not completed until 1963. It is still lightly used.

The small verdant farming area developed by the Mormons still exists in the heart of the park and provides an oasis of brilliant green in the desert setting of red and pink rock formations which constitutes most of the park area. It is a pleasing contrast, especially inasmuch as the campground has been placed in the middle of a peach orchard. Campers are even encouraged to help themselves to the peaches when they are ripe.

A short distance away from this green farmland, which is made possible by the Fremont River which winds through this section of the park, the arid desert climate closes in again, and the colors of the landscape turn to brilliant reds, pinks, tans, and whites.

The beauty of Capitol Reef National Park is in its groupings of warm-hued rocks, which are cut in strong, rugged blocks. It is a place of dignity and grandeur and great variety, with sheer walls, arches, and freestanding shapes whose strength can be felt on close terms because the approach roads lead right between the rocks, and the many foot trails permit one to walk into, around, and through many different kinds of formations.

For the amateur geologist Capitol Reef National Park is a dream come true. Up and down its slopes one can see clearly delineated the rock layers which were laid down age after age. Ultimately the layers were tilted up at an angle which then permitted uneven erosion, primarily by water. As the National Park Service folder which describes the area points out, water has been responsible, in one form or another, for the spectacular scenery in the park.

> Water, in the form of rivers carrying tremendous loads of stones, pebbles and grit, ground away at rocks and cliffs to carve the valleys. Water, as glaciers, helped grind the rocks and boulders into soil. Water, as ice, also created the pressures which split rocks to start the processes that made the soil beneath your feet. Water, as rain, softened and eroded the hard materials and transported them to other areas.

For those who want a sense of personal identification with the natural forces that have shaped the continent, there is no finer place to visit than Capitol Reef National Park. Because of its relatively light use, Park Service personnel here are generous in permitting visitors to enjoy the park without the restrictions one would find in more developed and heavily used areas. Visitors respond to this hospitality by treating the park with care and affection. The twelve foot trails through the area vary in length and difficulty, so that there is something for everyone.

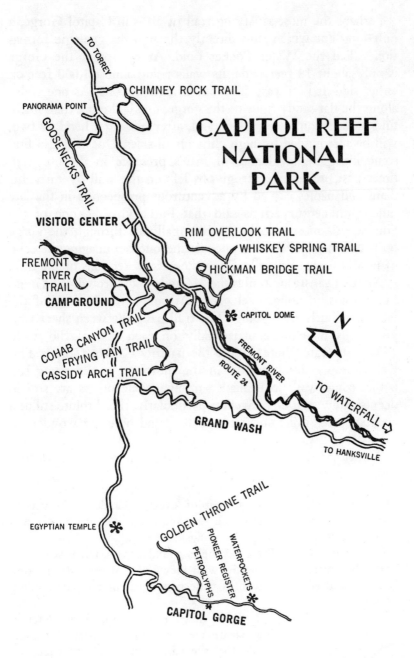

TO TORREY

CHIMNEY ROCK TRAIL

PANORAMA POINT

GOOSENECKS TRAIL

CAPITOL REEF NATIONAL PARK

VISITOR CENTER

RIM OVERLOOK TRAIL

WHISKEY SPRING TRAIL

FREMONT RIVER TRAIL

HICKMAN BRIDGE TRAIL

CAMPGROUND

CAPITOL DOME

COHAB CANYON TRAIL

FRYING PAN TRAIL

FREMONT RIVER

CASSIDY ARCH TRAIL

ROUTE 24

N

TO WATERFALL

GRAND WASH

TO HANKSVILLE

GOLDEN THRONE TRAIL

EGYPTIAN TEMPLE

WATERPOCKETS

PIONEER REGISTER

PETROGLYPHS

CAPITOL GORGE

Perhaps the most satisfying trail of all is in Capitol Gorge, a mile-long cut which runs directly through the geologic formation called the Water Pocket Fold. At one point the Gorge is only about 18 feet wide, its walls rising almost 1,000 feet on either side. It is an easy hike but an exciting one. As one walks along the flat sandy floor of the gorge, one will more than likely find oneself completely alone and, after making a bend or two, will be surrounded by high cliffs on all sides. One will also find some intriguing evidences of man's presence in the gorge in times past, including petroglyphs left on the wall by early Indians and names carved by adventurous prospectors in the late nineteenth century. It is said that Butch Cassidy, one of the Southwest's most colorful bandits, galloped through the gorge on occasion while eluding pursuit, and one can imagine the echo of hoofbeats as one walks along the narrow sections of the trail.

Another satisfying trail is the 2¼-mile hike through the Grand Wash—mostly along level ground through the bottom of the wash and fairly easy going. The trail passes between sheer canyon walls which rise majestically on each side of the wash, widely separated here, unlike the narrow Capitol Gorge. This walk is especially beautiful in the morning, as the rising sun bathes some walls in brilliant sunshine while others are still in deep shadow. For city dwellers particularly, the absolute stillness and complete isolation that can be found here are wonders in themselves.

Ten other trails are also available for hiking without restriction:

Goosenecks Trail, round trip of less than 1 mile. An easy walk with views of Sulphur Creek Canyon, handsome panoramas, and interesting rock formations alongside the trail.

Chimney Rock Trail, 3½ miles round trip. A fairly strenuous climb rewarding the hardy with views of Chimney Rock from below and above, as well as wide panoramas of the surrounding country.

Hickman Bridge Trail, 2 miles round trip. A moderately strenuous self-guiding nature trail, ending at a natural bridge. Signs along the trail identify the various trees, plants, cacti, archaeological remains, and significant natural formations. A trail guide is available for ten cents at the visitors' center which gives helpful descriptions of the interesting flora and fauna that can be seen along the way.

Whiskey Spring Trail, 3 miles round trip. A moderately strenuous hike which provides a view of Hickman Natural Bridge from above and then goes on to a small spring set in a shady little canyon.

Rim Overlook Trail, 4½ miles round trip. A strenuous climb which ends on top of a 1,000-foot cliff, affording spectacular views to the east, west, south—and straight down.

Cohab Canyon Trail, 1¾ miles from one end to the other, through the area chosen by the Mormon polygamists as a hideout. A moderately strenuous climb to this hidden canyon high above the Fremont River, with overlooks providing panoramic views.

Cassidy Arch Trail, 3 miles round trip. A strenuous climb over steep terrain from the floor of Grand Wash to high cliffs, ending above and behind the arch named for Butch Cassidy.

Frying Pan Trail, 3 miles long. A strenuous route linking the Cohab Canyon and Cassidy Arch trails over the summit of the reef, with many ups and downs over canyons and slick rocks.

Fremont River Trail, 2½ miles round trip. A moderately strenuous climb to a spot overlooking the canyon and the valley.

Golden Throne Trail, 4 miles round trip. A fairly strenuous climb from the bottom of Capitol Gorge to the top of the cliffs and on to the base of Golden Throne, one of the highest elevations in the park, providing rugged scenic views in all directions.

It is well worth taking two or three days to visit Capitol Reef National Park for the opportunity to explore some of its trails and savor the striking beauty of its rock formations and canyons. The visitors' center is well above average, with a good orientation film and well-done displays. The Park Rangers lead an 8:00 A.M. nature walk from the campground, and there is also a regular evening campfire talk.

One especially nice fringe benefit of a visit to this park is the waterfall in the Fremont River, along State 24, approximately 5 miles east of the visitors' center. At this spot the river cascades into a shallow pool about 4 feet deep. One can change into a bathing suit back in the campground, drive to a small parking area just 50 yards from the waterfall, walk down a sandy path to the pool, and enjoy a cool dip under and around the cascading water. In a part of the country where pools are few and far between, this one with its waterfall is a delightful treat.

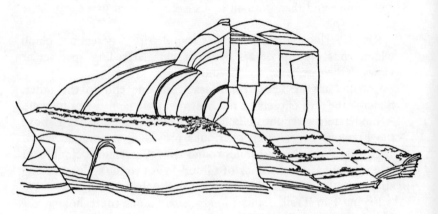

The Golden Throne (Capitol Reef National Park)

13
Dead Horse Point State Park (Utah)

Few people are aware that there are two Grand Canyons along the Colorado River. The second, lesser-known one is the Upper Grand Canyon, located northeast of Glen Canyon and Canyonlands. Because of its comparative remoteness, only a handful of people visit the area, and the result is that this natural wonder still arouses a full sense of excitement and discovery. In size, it is nowhere near so overwhelming as the Grand Canyon itself, but perhaps because of this it is easier to comprehend. The ideal spot for viewing and enjoying the Upper Grand Canyon is Dead Horse Point State Park. The park is reached by proceeding northwest from Moab, Utah, on U.S. 160 for approximately 10 miles to a road going off to the left which is marked by a prominent sign. This paved road runs approximately 23 miles directly to the park itself. The drive is exciting. There is a stretch of tight switchbacks which cause some apprehension but add to the adventure of the trip, and the balance of the way has many sights which fully repay the effort. There are dramatic rock formations, including sandstone shapes near the road which resemble frozen sand dunes complete with ridges and ripples; farther back from the road are sculptured stone cliffs and mesas. One long stretch of the drive traverses an area known as Big Flat,

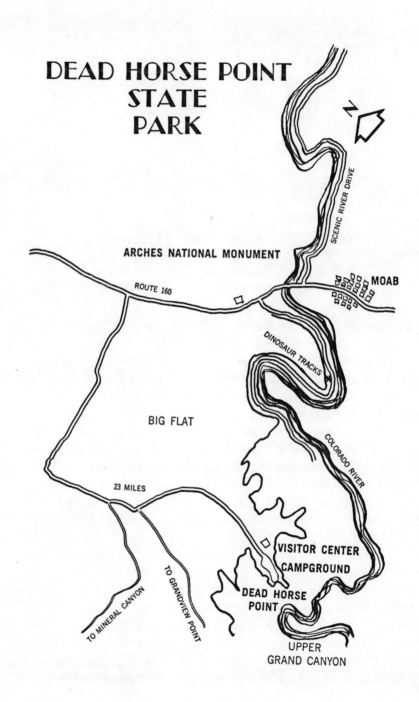

DEAD HORSE POINT STATE PARK

N

ARCHES NATIONAL MONUMENT

SCENIC RIVER DRIVE

MOAB

ROUTE 160

DINOSAUR TRACKS

BIG FLAT

COLORADO RIVER

23 MILES

TO MINERAL CANYON

TO GRANDVIEW POINT

VISITOR CENTER

CAMPGROUND

DEAD HORSE POINT

UPPER GRAND CANYON

a 90,000-acre livestock range. Cattle can frequently be seen along the road, sometimes ambling across in front of the car.

Near the end of the road, with a dramatic view of the Upper Grand Canyon, is the park visitors' center, an attractive building with clean conveniences. The outstanding feature of the Center is its museum, which may be one of the best museums of its kind in the Southwest. The portrayal of the stages of development of the area is clear and easy to understand. (The Utah State Department of Natural Resources deserves great credit for the high quality of this exhibit; in contrast, the display of the U.S. National Park Service at the North Rim of the Grand Canyon appears most amateurish.) Beyond the visitors' center the road leads on across a narrow neck of land to Dead Horse Point Park itself, with a parking area, visitors' shelter, and innumerable overlooks. The campground is presently located here, nestled in among rock ledges and cypress trees, with plenty of space between camping locations for privacy and a chance to enjoy the open space. The name of Dead Horse Point originates from the fact that the narrow neck leading to the point provided an ideal corral during the days when catching wild horses was part of the Western scene. According to the most generally accepted version, a large band of mustangs was once herded onto the point and a fence constructed across the narrow neck. After the best mustangs had been selected for sale, the balance were left to fend for themselves. Accounts differ as to whether the gate in the corral fence was left open or not, but in any event the confused horses wandered around in circles and large numbers eventually died of thirst in full view of the Colorado River below.

The view from Dead Horse Point covers 5,000 square miles of the Colorado Plateau, east as far as the La Sal Mountains, south to the Abajo Mountains, southwest to the Henry Mountains, and west to the Aquarius Plateau. The real view, however, is in the great gorge of the canyon itself. There the Colorado River flows through a maze of buttes and mesas and can be seen in a dozen places as it winds its way southwest, curving and looping at the bottom of the canyon, which is more than 2,000 feet deep. Visitors can view the chasm from any spot around Dead Horse Point, although a sitting wall is provided at the visitors' shelter expressly for the purpose. At other locations, one has to show considerable discretion in staying back from the edge of the canyon, which has no railing. There are views which give pleasure all through

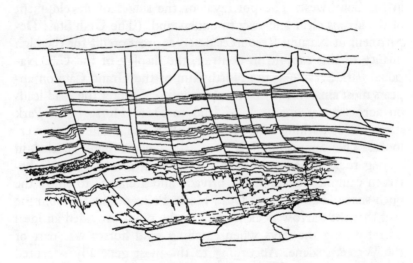

Upper Grand Canyon (Dead Horse Point State Park)

the day, but the finest are at sunset and sunrise. The sunsets in the Southwest are dramatic at almost any place, but from the edge of a yawning canyon they are overpowering. The changing hues and moods caused by the changing light and shadow bring a hush on all of nature.

In contrast to the subwaylike crowds on the various overlooks at the Grand Canyon to the southwest, overlooks of the Upper Grand Canyon can be quite lonely. One can take a walk, at dawn, to a point high above the river and not see another human being. Here in the absolute stillness of the early morning one can study birds soaring in space below the canyon rim and watch chipmunks scamper carelessly over rocks and ledges with thousand-foot drops only inches away. As the sun rises in the sky, the black shadows in the chasm give way to brilliant bands of color, as each level of sandstone is revealed. Then the sun seeks out the green growth along the river itself and makes it sparkle like an emerald necklace in the distance. At such a moment, man feels his true insignificance.

It is said that one of the special experiences one can have at Dead Horse Point is to stand near the rim of the canyon looking across it through a pair of binoculars, slowly dropping one's gaze down into the canyon until one is looking straight down at one's feet. It is a dizzying experience. The exercise generates a sensation of tumbling into the canyon itself, so that one is advised to have a companion along to provide a good grip if needed.

The views and the changing moods are the principal attraction of Dead Horse Point State Park, and a visit of one day is sufficient to enjoy it fully. But for those who would like to savor the excitement of a dramatic canyon view in personal terms, without the crowds of the other Grand Canyon and with sufficient opportunity to reflect on the meaning of human life in a world which has lasted for millions of years, Dead Horse Point is a must.

14
Great Sand Dunes
National Monument (Colorado)

There is a legend that a band of web-footed wild horses lives among the dunes at Great Sand Dunes National Monument. There may be some truth to the legend, for it has been reported that wild horses have been seen in the area which have developed hoofs that are broader than ordinary, apparently as natural compensation for the difficulty of moving in the sand. The Great Sand Dunes are a natural phenomenon and a curiosity, but they are more than that. They create a landscape of forever changing moods as the sun moves across the sky and the shadows on the dunes move with it, often overlaid with racing or slowly drifting cloud shadows, giving movement and form to the great windswept mass of sand which has accumulated here over many centuries.

It is hard for a visitor who first comes upon the sand dunes not to look around instinctively for the ocean. It is indeed a strange sight to see so much sand in the middle of an arid stretch of country rimmed by high mountains. There are several theories on how the sand became piled so high at the foot of these mountains. Because a large amount of volcanic material appears in the sand, it is reasoned that much of it came from the San Juan

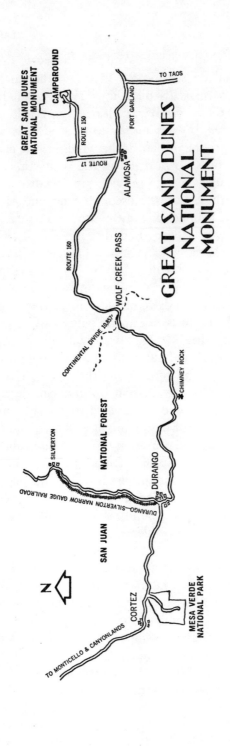

GREAT SAND DUNES
NATIONAL
MONUMENT

Mountains across the valley. Another theory is that there was once a great inland sea located here and that after the water evaporated, the sand was piled up by the wind. In any event the accumulation of sand was clearly the result of prevailing southwesterly winds carrying grains of sand toward the mountains and then dropping them as the winds hit the natural barrier, much as snow piles up in drifts in the wintertime. The Sangre de Cristo Mountains, which provide the backdrop for the dunes, are crossed by three passes, Mosca, Medano, and Music, through which the winds funnel as they continue on their course. The sand is too heavy to be carried through the mountains and so accumulates at the foot of the passes. The winds blow constantly, shaping and changing the dunes. When storms sweep down from the northeast, they shift the ridges in opposite directions, and then the southwest winds return and force the sands to reverse themselves. The result is a dramatic pattern of huge sand ridges, one behind the other. As shadows come across the face of the dunes, these ridges stand out in sharp relief, more handsome even than the more familiar dunes along the ocean shore.

The Great Sand Dunes National Monument deserves an overnight visit, which provides a chance to see the long afternoon shadows, the blanket of colored light at sunset, and the brilliance of the dawn light in the morning. The campground is sensibly located where it provides a splendid view of the dunes, both evening and morning, and although the attendance of visitors is fairly high, and the camping places are located closer together than at some other park grounds, the area still has a great natural feeling and is most enjoyable.

In addition to the unique scenic features of Great Sand Dunes National Monument, the dunes provide an unusual recreational facility, particularly for families traveling with children. Youngsters can have a great time in this enormous natural sandpile. They can climb and climb and climb to their hearts' content and then slide down the steep slopes into cushioned valleys below. The highest dunes rise as much as 700 feet, and although the sand is hot in the middle of the day it is quite comfortable in the early morning and late afternoon.

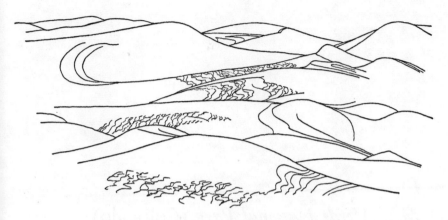

Great Sand Dunes National Monument

At the visitors' center, one can see evidences that the Great Sand Dunes also held a fascination for the Indians over many centuries. Archaeological studies indicate that nomadic hunters occupied the area 10,000 years ago, leaving some of the earliest traces of man's existence on this continent. Two early campsites have been excavated, yielding spear points and the bones of animals which appear to be an extinct species of bison.

The sands and their mysterious appearance, particularly by moonlight, have given rise to many folk tales of supernatural happenings. One story is told of a long wagon train which came through Mosca Pass during the early days of the pioneers. Camp was made for the night at the edge of the dunes. In the morning the teamsters awoke to discover that their mules and wagons had completely disappeared. It is probable that quicksands were the cause of the disappearance, but many people believe that supernatural forces were responsible.

There are two approach roads to the monument. One is State 150 off State 17, north of Mosca, Colorado. This is a paved road all the way into the monument. The other route proceeds north from U.S. 160, 5 miles west of Blanca. This is a dirt road, corrugated by heavy use and not advisable for those who are traveling with trailers because the vibrations can wreak havoc with the contents of a trailer.

15
Mesa Verde National Park (Colorado)

One day in 1888, two cattlemen, Richard Wetherill and Charlie Mason, were riding across the tableland on top of the large mesa overlooking Montezuma Valley. When they came to the edge of a deep canyon, they paused and looked across at the canyon's opposite wall. To their amazement the two men saw what appeared to be an apartment house made of gold, constructed right in the face of the cliff. What they had actually discovered was the great abandoned cliff dwellers' structure now known as Cliff Palace. As far as can be determined, they were the first outsiders to view the structure since it had been vacated by its former tenants six centuries before.

Word of the discovery of the cliff dwelling excited great interest in the scientific community. In 1891, a Swedish expedition conducted extensive explorations at Mesa Verde, excavating many of the ruins and assembling a large collection of Indian pottery and artifacts, which were packed up and shipped off to Sweden. This treasure of archaeological remains was intended to be displayed at the Royal Museum in Stockholm, but instead it moldered away in warehouses for half a century until finally in 1938 the collection was sent to a museum in Helsinki.

Other "pothunters" helped themselves to treasures at Mesa

Verde over the next decade and a half until finally, in 1906, Congress enacted the Federal Antiquities Act prohibiting the removal of historic artifacts. In that same year, Mesa Verde was designated as one of the nation's first national parks.

In marked contrast to the six centuries when no outsiders visited Mesa Verde, today the place is jammed with visitors. Waiting lines for tickets to visit the principal ruins are long, waiting periods may run four to six hours, and the pushing and shoving and loud commentary at the various locations is disheartening. Nevertheless, no conscientious traveler can visit the Southwest without seeing Mesa Verde National Park. The key is to find the real pleasures and enjoyment that a visit can provide, notwithstanding the crowds.

Despite the huge numbers they must accommodate, the camping facilities at Mesa Verde are surprisingly nice. Morfield Campground, 4 miles inside the park, has space for almost 500 campers, yet the campsites are well spaced and generally quite attractive. The service facilities at Morfield Village are outstanding. In addition to coin-operated washing machines and showers, there is an excellent store which stocks not only a full range of foodstuffs but also as good a supply of camping equipment as one is likely to find anywhere. In addition, there is a first-rate gift shop which has a wide range of Indian arts and crafts of unusually high quality at what appear to be reasonable prices.

The campfire programs, although held in an amphitheater which resembles a junior Hollywood Bowl, are occasionally capped off by ceremonial dances performed by Navajo park employees. If one is fortunate enough to witness one of these dances, accompanied by falsetto-voice chants to staccato rhythms, he will carry away a haunting memory of sights and sounds. The dance program is marred somewhat by the passing of baskets for contributions, which not only delays the performance but also spoils the natural and uncommercial approach of the dancers themselves. It would seem to be better judgment on the part of the Park Service if some portion of the campground fee were applied to a bonus payment for the Indian performers.

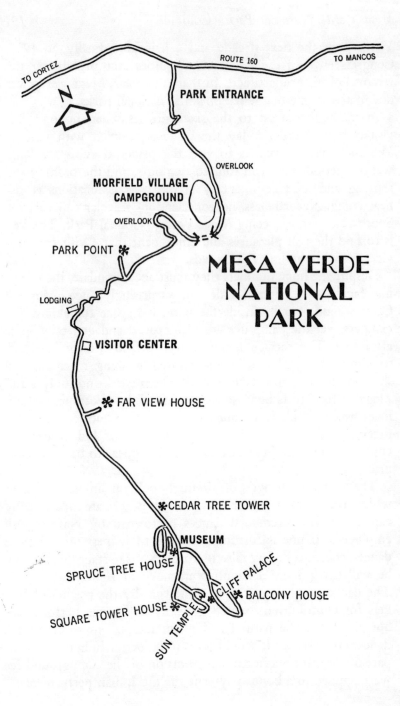

TO CORTEZ

ROUTE 160

TO MANCOS

PARK ENTRANCE

N

OVERLOOK

MORFIELD VILLAGE CAMPGROUND

OVERLOOK

PARK POINT ✳

MESA VERDE NATIONAL PARK

LODGING

◻ **VISITOR CENTER**

✳ **FAR VIEW HOUSE**

✳ **CEDAR TREE TOWER**

MUSEUM

SPRUCE TREE HOUSE

CLIFF PALACE

✳ **BALCONY HOUSE**

SQUARE TOWER HOUSE ✳

SUN TEMPLE

In the campground area is a stable where group horseback riding trips are organized at regular intervals throughout the day. These trips are among the special pleasures of a visit to Mesa Verde, and anyone with enough spunk to climb on to the back of a strange steed in strange country, should be sure to take one. Despite the fact that portions of the trail seem a little precarious, the horses have traveled back and forth so often that they could undoubtedly make the trip safely while sound asleep. The regular hour-long trip goes out along the face of the mesa, with a dramatic view of the farming country below and sometimes perhaps a glimpse of the nest of a golden eagle. (Incidentally, this same trail, called "Knife Edge Trail," is also excellent for hiking on foot, particularly in the early morning.) The two-hour horseback ride climbs up a fairly steep trail, with several switchbacks, to the very top of the mesa.

Despite the crowded conditions in other parts of the park, there are at least five somewhat less populated spots that can be visited with great enjoyment: the fire lookout ranger station, the new visitors' center, the Archaeological Museum, the Ruins Drive, and Far View House.

The principal archaeological area in Mesa Verde National Park is 20 miles from the park entrance and involves some fairly exciting driving, although the road is an excellent blacktop. Halfway along this road is Park Point, the highest spot on the mesa, with an altitude of 8,572 feet. Right at the peak is a ranger station, with a 360-degree view in all directions. There is also a lookout point where visitors can view the edges of the mesa and the landscape below. This is one of the rare chances to observe a ranger station at close hand, and, although visitors are not permitted inside the station itself, it is possible to get a good feeling for what it is like just by looking through the glass. Chances are that the ranger on duty will welcome the chance to vary an otherwise routine day by answering some questions about flora and fauna or other topics of interest.

A few miles farther on is the circular modern visitors' center at Navajo Hill, which was opened in 1968. For some reason this facility is not crowded with visitors, and it is possible to spend upward of an hour here in peace and quiet. The displays portray principally Indian silver and pottery. In contrast to the main museum, which is done in the old style of exhibition, the latest techniques in museum display have been used at the visitors' center, including brilliant spotlighting of the carefully selected exhibits and dramatic colored backgrounds. This is undoubtedly one of the best interpretations of Indian pottery and jewelry in the Southwest and should not be missed if one wants to learn something about the arts and crafts of the area.

The main Archaeological Museum at Chapin Mesa is a sleeper. Everything about it is discouraging at first appearance. It is old-style, down at the heels, and appears quite gloomy when you first arrive. But after a few minutes of examination, the contents of the exhibit cases come to life, and it is apparent that this is unquestionably as exciting an archaeological display as one could ever hope to find.

At the heart of the excellent displays at the Chapin Mesa Museum is the group of dioramas portraying the various stages of Indian development and life. These three-dimensional models are enchanting and surpass any comparable dioramas one is likely to see, even at the Smithsonian Institution in Washington. The secret of the success of the Mesa Verde dioramas is the variety and interest of the contents of each scene, combined with the natural stances and positions of the miniature human figures. Everybody seems to be doing something, or at least showing a reaction that seems natural and lifelike. Simply as portrayals of human activity, the dioramas are sheer delight. But they are more than that, for they really do explain, in terms that no other technique could, how the various Pueblo Indians lived in the Southwest over the course of centuries.

In addition to the superb dioramas, there are other displays at the Archaeological Museum which deserve close attention. The cases containing artifacts are a little quaint in their lettering and portrayal, but the content is so rich in interest that one quickly overlooks these drawbacks. One particularly fascinating exhibit is a medicine man's bag, perfectly preserved with all of its contents for over a thousand years. The bag and its contents are laid out on a display board where one can examine each piece from only a few inches away. Included are such curious things as a dried human thumb; porcupine teeth; a weasel skin containing five arrowheads; five galena (lead ore) crystals in a skin wrapper; five shell and four stone beads; a weasel skin bag with a hawk's claw attached, and the serpentine pipe it contained; a buckskin wrapper containing eleven pieces of turquoise; a leather wrapper containing two rolls of skin, each decorated with beads and parrot feathers; another leather wrapper containing a disc of abalone shell, and on and on. Although we smile at these things in the age of penicillin, it is worth reflecting on the fact that many of the Indian rituals and chants are still used today to cure the sick and continue to have a large measure of success because they are rooted in the psychological approach of developing a desire to get well.

Another exhibit at the Mesa Verde Archaeological Museum, which will fascinate amateur detectives, is the explanation of the tree-ring dating procedure used by archaeologists to determine the precise years when certain ruins were originally constructed. An unusual form of slide rule has been constructed which permits easy calculation of the actual growing period of any piece of wood found in the Southwest over the course of many centuries.

The greatest discovery of all, if you are attuned to such things, is the beauty of the early pottery designs. The display cases show samples of pottery made in the various centuries, climaxing in the classic Pueblo Period between A.D. 1100 and 1300. Probably the most dramatic single exhibit at the Archaeological Museum is a case containing a large pottery storage jar in which were found twenty-two quarts of corn, perfectly preserved for over 700 years. The reason was that the mouth of the storage jar had been covered by a small bowl which had been turned upside down to protect the contents from the elements. One is first struck by the wonder of seeing corn kernels exactly the same as those we see on our own dinner plates each summer, and then one's attention turns to the jar. The pattern of decoration, both on the jar and on the small bowl, is extraordinarily handsome in its simplicity and discipline. Particularly if you appreciate modern art forms, the potter's restraint in leaving certain areas unpainted while others are lavishly decorated commands immediate appreciation.

Other display cases nearby contain additional examples of pottery art of the classic period. The shapes are beautiful in themselves, but the disciplined black-on-white patterns which have been painted on the surface as decoration are simply superb. Given the technical limitations of the time, here is an art form which matches any of the finest work of abstract graphic artists today. Not every visitor will share the same reaction, but those who are sensitive to art movements are bound to be filled with the excitement of discovery which is present in this dusty, old-fashioned museum.

Behind the Archaeological Museum is one of the largest cliff dwellings in Mesa Verde National Park, Spruce Tree House. Unlike the ruins at Cliff Palace and Balcony House, which require tickets and involve long waits, Spruce Tree House can be visited simply by following a self-guiding trail down to the cave in which the house was built. The house is 216 feet long and approximately 89 feet wide and was a self-contained village

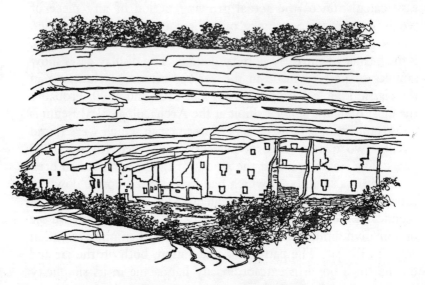

Spruce Tree House (Mesa Verde National Park)

with an estimated population of two hundred inhabiting its 122 rooms, including 8 kivas and 14 storage rooms. Originally the walls rose to the top of the cave, which served as a roof for the upper chambers. The masonry work is exceptionally fine and well preserved.

The Ruins Drive consists of two self-guiding loops, each covering approximately 6 miles, along which there are a number of stopping points where cliff dwellings can be viewed from the canyon rim and some mesa-top ruins can be visited. As already noted, the most publicized sites at Mesa Verde are almost impossible to visit except as part of a crowded tour group, usually after long hours of waiting. Cliff Palace, the most beautiful, can be seen from an overview near the ticket counter at the edge of the canyon rim, and a pair of binoculars will give the visitor almost as satisfying a visual trip into the ruins as climbing down the ladder itself. Balcony House is not visible from the canyon rim, and there are stern warnings to those who are frail, or faint of heart, that the climb down and back is strenuous.

Along the road returning toward the park entrance about 4 miles from the museum is Far View House, reached by a short side road which also leads to Pipe Shrine House. These are both mesa-top pueblos constructed 800 to 1,000 years ago. The advantage of visiting these ruins is that they are seldom crowded, and one can climb up short ladders and walk along the tops of the walls in order to examine the various rooms. The large ceremonial kiva in Far View House is a particularly good example of this special cultural facility and is fascinating to walk around. None of the discomforts of being herded like sheep or having to wait for tour tickets apply here.

A sensible way to budget one's time at Mesa Verde National Park is to arrive late one day, in time to set up camp and have supper, and possibly do some shopping at Morfield Village. Early the following morning, leaving camp gear behind, one can drive the full distance to the ruins, the museum, and the visitors' center, returning to the campground at the end of the day. One might top the visit off with an early morning horseback trail ride before heading on to the next stop.

16
Zion National Park (Utah)

As one stands on the banks of the Virgin River, it is hard to conceive how this small muddy stream could possibly have cut through five thousand feet of rock to create the dramatic peaks and cliffs which today make up Zion National Park. Closer examination, however, discloses that the water is loaded with small grains of rock, moving at a fast pace because of the sharp incline of the stream bed. For this reason, the Virgin River is often described as "a moving ribbon of sandpaper." This muddy stream, even today, carries away more than a million tons of rock wastes every year. Although the current seems fairly restrained on a dry day, when the floods come from heavy rains, the velocity and volume of the river increase many times, to the point where large boulders can be moved and walls scraped high above the stream bed.

The Paiute Indians knew Zion Canyon as Arrow Quiver (the Indian word was *ioogoon*). The first white man to discover the canyon was Nephi Johnson, a Mormon pioneer, who went there in 1858. Johnson was followed shortly by farmers and cattlemen who moved into the area to establish farms and ranches, and whose descendants continued to occupy the area until it was designated a national park. The Mormons found a welcome sanctuary in the canyon, which the Indians feared and left alone. The small Mormon settlement was originally called Little Zion. It is said that when Brigham Young told the settlers that the valley was *not* Zion they renamed it Not Zion.

Part of the area was placed under protection by President Taft in 1909. The public land area was later enlarged by President Wilson in 1918 and finally designated as a national park by Congress in 1929.

There are no words to describe the scenic beauty of Zion National Park. You have to see it for yourself. The mood of the place is probably best described by the ecclesiastical names which have been given to many of the prominent peaks and geological features, such as the Temple, the Organ, the Pulpit, the Three Patriarchs, and Angels Landing. There is indeed something cathedral-like about the park. The towering dignity of the canyon walls conveys a sense of solemnity and reverence. Every turn in the park road reveals some new vista of a great spire or cliff which soars heavenward.

The approach to Zion National Park, particularly from the east, is an experience in itself. The scenery grows more and more rugged and striking after one passes the park entrance. Of particular notice is Checkerboard Mesa. Then there is a long black tunnel, running for more than a mile, with a few scattered portholes along the sides, through which blinding sunlight streams. At the end of the tunnel—which was drilled straight through the red sandstone—one suddenly comes into Zion Canyon and begins the steep descent, with its half dozen switchbacks from which one can glimpse awesome views of the canyon walls in all directions.

The visitors' center is superb. There is a large-scale relief map of the canyon area on which one can trace the various trails. There is a fairly good introductory lecture in the form of a slide show, and there is a very good nature museum. The museum includes interesting exhibits on the wild life and plant life in the area, as well as well-designed geological exhibits. One of the best of the latter is a group of rock specimens which one can touch and even pick up—the best possible way to learn rock identifica-

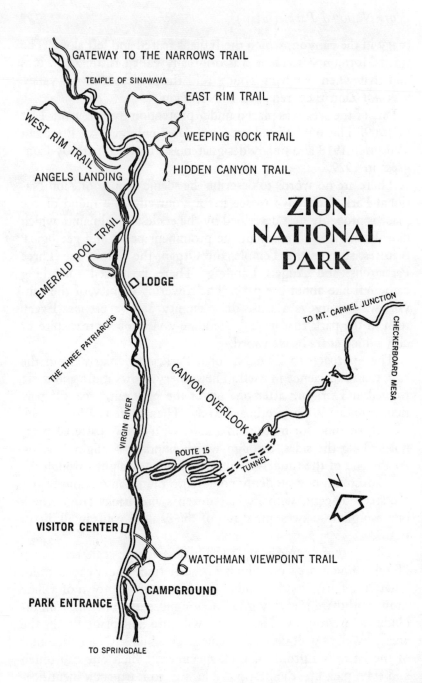

GATEWAY TO THE NARROWS TRAIL

TEMPLE OF SINAWAVA

EAST RIM TRAIL

WEST RIM TRAIL

WEEPING ROCK TRAIL

ANGELS LANDING

HIDDEN CANYON TRAIL

ZION NATIONAL PARK

EMERALD POOL TRAIL

LODGE

TO MT. CARMEL JUNCTION

CHECKERBOARD MESA

THE THREE PATRIARCHS

CANYON OVERLOOK

VIRGIN RIVER

ROUTE 15

TUNNEL

N

VISITOR CENTER

WATCHMAN VIEWPOINT TRAIL

CAMPGROUND

PARK ENTRANCE

TO SPRINGDALE

tion. The campground facilities have recently been enlarged so that there are plenty of camping spaces available, including many locations along the bank of the Virgin River, which flows through this part of the park. The campgrounds are encircled by rugged peaks which are beautiful at all times of the day. For those who have been on the road for several days, there is a coin laundry in the town of Springdale, just outside the south entrance to the park, not far from the campground.

Because Zion National Park is popular, the campfire programs must accommodate a substantial number of people and have therefore grown quite impersonal. The reliance on color slides is probably a necessity, but it tends to demoralize the ranger who speaks, and his feeling of boredom and loss of initiative often come through in his voice and manner.

One of the surprising side benefits of a stay at Zion is that campers are welcome to use the large swimming pool at the lodge simply by paying a modest swimming fee. A cool swim in this lovely setting, with high red peaks on all sides, is memorable.

The park drive to the Temple of Sinawava is splendid. There are several dramatic views from drive-offs along the way, and the mood and drama of the Temple of Sinawava itself are spectacular.

There are a number of foot trails in Zion National Park, the most noted of which is the trail from the parking lot at the Temple of Sinawava to the Gateway to the Narrows. This is an easily covered 2-mile round trip with no steep grades, which provides a fine view of the river flood plain and the narrowing space between the canyon walls.

Weeping Rock Trail is only ½ mile long and is an easy self-guided walk to the overhanging cliff with its dripping water, hanging gardens, and travertine deposits.

The Emerald Pool Trail is 2 miles long, moderately easy, and provides a chance to see a lovely small pool formed by two waterfalls.

Overlook Trail, about 1 mile long, is mostly easy walking to the top of the Great Arch, from which there is an excellent view of Pine Creek Canyon and the west side of Zion Canyon.

Watchman Viewpoint Trail is about 2 miles long and is also moderately easy. It offers a view of the Watchman, Zion, and Oak Creek Canyon.

The East Rim Trail is a fairly strenuous foot and horse trail

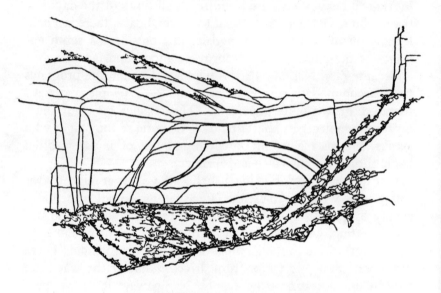

Great Arch (Zion National Park)

which should only be undertaken by the hardy. The Trail is 7 miles long round trip and involves climbs of over 2,000 feet. It requires at least five hours to traverse.

Hidden Canyon Trail is another fairly strenuous hike, covering 2 miles round trip and climbing 850 feet. The end of the trail is well worth the effort, for Hidden Canyon is an almost inaccessible place of quiet and solitude.

West Rim Trail is the most strenuous trail in the park. It climbs more than 3,000 feet up, covers 12½ miles round trip, and requires eight hours to cover.

Angels Landing Trail is also strenuous and should be attempted by experienced hikers only. There is a steep climb of almost 1,500 feet. The entire trail covers 5 miles and requires four hours to hike, but it rewards those sturdy enough to attempt it with a spectacular view of Zion Canyon.

Although a great many people visit Zion National Park, one does not have the sense of being crowded, primarily because there is so much room to roam. The nobility of the scenery and the excellence of the facilities make Zion one of the best places to visit in the Southwest.

Angels Landing (Zion National Park)

17
The Indian Reservations

On July 4, 1776, while the Continental Congress was busily signing the Declaration of Independence in Philadelphia, a Spanish priest named Fray Francisco Garcés sat beside his saddle in the plaza of an Indian village two thirds of a continent away, patiently hoping to work out a peaceful agreement between the Spaniards and the Hopi Indians. The plaza was in the middle of the ancient village of Oraibi, in country which is now Arizona. Father Garcés had been sitting patiently in the same spot for two days, and no one had spoken to him throughout that time. His guides had long since taken flight and left him to fend for himself. The Hopis had killed the last Spanish missionary priest almost a century before. But the courageous Garcés hoped to reach a new accord with them.

As the day wore on, a crowd gathered menacingly. Then four of the head men came forward and told the priest to leave immediately. His mule was brought forward, and he saddled up and rode off. Father Garcés had expected to be killed when he saw the crowd gathering, but the Hopis, apparently impressed by his patience and endurance, had decided to let him go. He was the last white man with the temerity to try to affect the destiny of this fiercely independent tribe.

Oraibi still stands on the Arizona desert, still inhabited by Hopi Indians who still keep the white man at arm's length. It would be a mistake for a visitor to believe that he would be any more welcome in Oraibi today than Father Garcés was in 1776. Times have not changed much for this ancient tribe which has inhabited the Southwest for almost fifteen centuries. Their customs and traditions run counter to the white man's civilization, and they resist outside intrusions with a stubbornness that must be admired.

Anyone with more than a passing interest in the history of the American continent would cheat himself out of a worthwhile experience if he did not make it a special point to visit the great Indian reservations of the Southwest and see for himself what life there is like. Not only will he find that most Indians resent and resist the intrusions of modern civilization, but he will also begin to understand the basis for the claims of injustice on behalf of the Indian tribes whose land and hunting grounds were taken away by settlers, backed by the United States Army, a century ago amid much bloodshed and hardship.

There are five major Indian tribes located in the Southwest. Far and away the most significant are the Navajos, whose reservation covers hundreds of square miles in northeastern Arizona plus some lands in Utah and New Mexico. Second most important are the Hopis, followed by the Rio Grande Pueblo Indians, the Zuñis, and the Utes. All have reservations which can be visited, although they are not necessarily all scenic.

THE NAVAJO INDIAN RESERVATION

There are a number of excellent paved roads crisscrossing the Navajo reservation and many interesting things to be seen there. As already noted in Chapter 10, Canyon de Chelly National Monument is one of the most delightful places to visit in the entire Southwest and plays a major role as the traditional heartland of the Navajos. Other important landmarks include Monument Valley, a striking display of mesas, spires, and geologic formations located in the northern part of the reservation, ap-

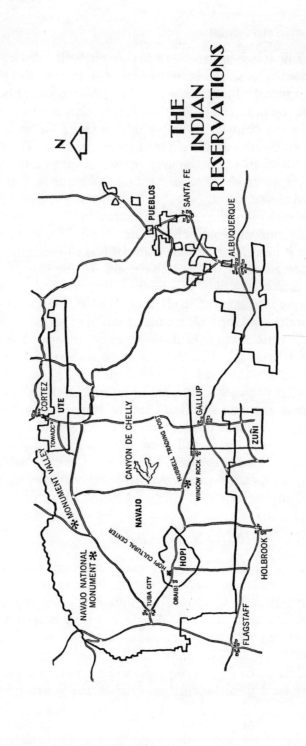

THE
INDIAN
RESERVATIONS

N

PUEBLOS

SANTA FE

ALBUQUERQUE

CORTEZ

UTE

TOWAOC

MONUMENT VALLEY

CANYON DE CHELLY

HUBBELL TRADING POST

GALLUP

ZUÑI

WINDOW ROCK

NAVAJO

NAVAJO NATIONAL
MONUMENT

HOPI CULTURAL CENTER

TUBA CITY

ORAIBI

HOPI

HOLBROOK

FLAGSTAFF

proximately 25 miles north of Kayenta, Arizona, and the Navajo National Monument, about 25 miles southwest of Kayenta, where there are three large well-preserved prehistoric cliff dwellings.

Probably the most interesting spot to visit, apart from Canyon de Chelly, is Window Rock, Arizona (not far from Gallup, New Mexico), the tribal headquarters for the reservation. In addition to the headquarters structures and the unusual rock formation from which it gets its name, Window Rock also offers

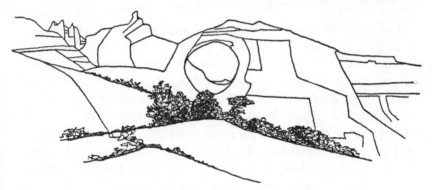

Window Rock (Navajo Reservation)

a reasonably good tribal museum plus the excellent main headquarters of the Navajo Arts and Crafts Guild, where one can purchase Navajo silver, rugs, and other handicrafts at fair prices and with confidence. Window Rock can be visited easily en route to Canyon de Chelly. Also along this same route is the Hubbell Trading Post at Ganado, Arizona, which has been designated a National Historic Site. Hubbell Trading Post, which is still in operation, was run for ninety years by John Lorenzo Hubbell and his family. Hubbell, who had been a Spanish interpreter and had become familiar with the ways of the Navajos, began trading with the Indians at Ganado in 1876. Two years later he bought out the man who had previously owned the big trading post there. Because of Hubbell's special rapport with the

Navajos, his trading post became the center of commercial and social activity for Indians who came from miles around. Hubbell was not only a merchant but also a special ambassador between the Indian and the white man. He translated and wrote letters, arbitrated disputes, interpreted government policy, and provided health services. His heroic efforts during a smallpox epidemic on the reservation in 1886 won him the lasting admiration and gratitude of the Navajos. In time, Hubbell's commercial operations expanded to fourteen trading posts as well as a stage and freight line, making him unquestionably the most important trader in the Navajo country.

Hubbell's principal contribution, however, was that of encouraging the development of Navajo arts and crafts. He set a standard of excellence in craftsmanship, insisting on a high level of quality which undoubtedly contributed to the successful flowering of the Navajo talents. A trading post is often a combination of pawnshop, bank, and grocery store. The Navajos bring in rugs and silver to be exchanged for credit to buy provisions and goods. The Hubbell Trading Post at Ganado was a great favorite with the Indians because of Hubbell's interest in their work, and they looked forward to their visits there as one might look forward to a vacation trip. Trading was lengthy, with much conversation, and much good-natured exchange with other Indians who had come to the trading post. Stories were exchanged around the stove, problems discussed, and news and gossip traded along with the merchandise and jewelry.

Hubbell also influenced the design of Navajo work, particularly the rugs. He arranged to have a number of rug designs painted in reduced scale by a visiting artist, E. A. Burbank, which the Indians could then copy in enlarged form as rugs. Today one can still see many of these early designs developed under Hubbell's supervision, as well as some of the rugs which have been produced from them.

Because of the language barrier, the labels on canned goods gained a special significance in commerce with the Indians. Once an Indian became accustomed to purchasing according to a certain type of label, the trader could not safely change brands.

There is a story told of one unfortunate trader who purchased a large stock of Carnation evaporated milk and sustained heavy losses because the Indians refused to believe that a can with a flower on the label could contain milk.

More detailed information about the Navajos and places to visit on the Navajo Reservation may be obtained by writing to the Parks and Recreation Department, Navajo Tribe, Window Rock, Ariz. 86515.

THE HOPI INDIAN RESERVATION

The Hopi reservation is located right in the middle of the Navajo reservation. It consists of three large mesas on which are located a number of small villages. Each village has its own separate leadership and its own special identity and customs. Generally speaking, visitors will not feel welcome at these villages and would be better advised to observe them at a respectful distance. The one exception is the Hopi Cultural Center on Second Mesa, opened in the spring of 1971 and specifically planned to interpret current Hopi activities for the benefit of outsiders. Next door is the Hopi Silvercraft Guild, founded after World War II, when a group of Hopi veterans took advantage of the G.I. Bill of Rights to get training in silver work and developed a special art form utilizing overlays which now can be clearly identified as Hopi silverwork. The guild is probably the best place to see Hopi silver, as well as other arts and crafts, and to make purchases at prices which are fair and reliable.

One of the goals of knowledgeable visitors to the Southwest has always been to see the Hopi Snake Dance in late August. For many years outsiders were permitted to observe this important religious ceremony. In time, however, the inevitable occurred, and growing abuses of the privilege by thoughtless tourists generated increasing ill will. Finally, in 1971, the Hopis banned all white people from attendance at the Snake Dance. The basis for the decision to ban outsiders is instructive, for it shows how distant the Indian and surrounding cultures are from each other and shows also how zealously the Hopis guard their traditions. The following is the full text of a mimeographed handbill distributed by the Hopi Indians to anyone who approached the site of the 1971 Snake Dance. The text was also sent as a letter to the chambers of commerce in the principal nearby cities outside the reservation area.

HOPI INDEPENDENT NATION
MISHONGNOVI VILLAGE
SECOND MESA, ARIZONA
AUGUST 8, 1971

CHAMBER OF COMMERCE
WINSLOW, HOLEBROOK, FLAGSTAFF, ARIZONA
TO HOPI PEOPLE

DEAR SIR:

ON BEHALF OF MY HOPI PEOPLE AND MEMBERS OF THE ORDER OF ANTELOPE AND SNAKE SOCIETY IN THE VILLAGE OF MISHONGNOVI ON SECOND MESA AND IN ORDER TO PRESERVE, MAINTAIN AND TRULY PROTECT OUR SACRED RELIGIOUS CEREMONIES, OUR CULTURE AND LAND, I, STARLIE LOMAYAKTEWA, VILLAGE KIKMONGI, TODAY ANNOUNCE TO YOU, THE WORLD IN GENERAL AND TO OUR HOPI PEOPLE THAT WE ARE CLOSING OUR HOPI ANTELOPE AND SNAKE CEREMONY TO *ALL WHITE PEOPLE* THIS YEAR FOR THE FOLLOWING REASONS:

1. TO THE HOPI PEOPLE ANTELOPE AND SNAKE CEREMONY IS ONE OF THE MOST SACRED OF ALL OF OUR CEREMONIES AND MUST BE RESPECTED AND GUARDED AS SUCH BY ALL PEOPLE. IN THE PAST MANY OF OUR OWN HOPI PEOPLE AS WELL AS OUR INDIAN FRIENDS WHO COME TO PARTICIPATE IN A PRAYER FOR RAIN, ABUNDANCE OF FOOD AND LONG LIFE FOR ALL LIVING THINGS ON THIS EARTH ARE CROWDED OUT BY SO MANY WHITE TOURS AND STUDENTS WHO SEEMED TO HAVE NO RESPECT FOR OUR SACRED RITUALS.

2. IN SPITE OF OUR REPEATED WARNINGS AND ANNOUNCEMENTS THAT WE DO NOT ALLOW PICTURES, HAND DRAWINGS AND RECORDINGS DURING THE CEREMONY YET SOMEONE IS ALWAYS DOING THAT THEREBY CREATING MUCH RESENTMENT AMONG OUR HOPI PEOPLE AND DISTURBING THE CEREMONIAL DANCERS. TODAY WE FOUND THAT CHAMBER OF COMMERCE PEOPLE IN PRESCOTT, ARIZONA, AND OTHER WHITE PEOPLE ARE NOW USING OUR SACRED CEREMONIES FOR COMMERCIAL PURPOSES. THIS MUST BE STOPPED.

3. MANY OF OUR HOUSES IN THE VILLAGE ARE VERY OLD AND CANNOT HOLD UP SO MANY PEOPLE COMING UP ON THE HOUSE TOPS. IT ENDANGERS THE HOUSES AND THE PEOPLE.

4. THIS CEREMONY IS NOT AN ENTERTAINMENT OR A SHOW FOR THE WHITE PEOPLE WHO HAVE NO RESPECT FOR OUR CEREMONIES. WE HAVE THE BUREAU OF INDIAN AFFAIRS, THE SO-CALLED HOPI TRIBAL COUNCIL AND THE HOUSING AUTHORITIES TO BUILD 60-UNIT HOUSING PROJECT RIGHT IN OUR MOST SACRED RELIGIOUS GROUNDS BELOW OUR MESA. THIS MUST BE STOPPED ALSO.

5. BECAUSE MANY OF OUR SACRED OBJECTS, SUCH AS PRAYER FEATHERS, SHRINES HAVE BEEN DISTURBED AND EVEN TAKEN AWAY BY WHITE PEOPLE WE ASK THE MEMBERS OF THE CHAMBER OF COMMERCE AND THE SO-CALLED HOPI TRIBAL COUNCIL TO STOP BRINGING WHITE TOURS TO OUR SACRED CEREMONIES.

6. I ASK ALL HOPI PEOPLE TO HELP US TO PROTECT AND RESPECT OUR OWN RELIGIOUS CEREMONIES FROM NOW ON. LET THERE BE NO DRINKING OF INTOXICATING LIQUOR IN THE VILLAGE DURING THE CEREMONY. I APPEAL TO ALL OF OUR YOUNG MEN TO COME AND HELP US TO SEE THAT OUR DEMANDS ARE RESPECTED. IF ANYONE WISHING TO HELP PLEASE CONTACT US AS SOON AS POS-

SIBLE. ANYONE FOUND DISTURBING THIS CERE-
MONY WILL BE BROUGHT BEFORE THE COMBINED
ANTELOPE AND SNAKE MEMBERS IMMEDIATELY
AFTER THE CONCLUSION OF THE RITUAL.
VILLAGE LEADER   (SIGNED)

STARLIE LOMAYAKTEWA

OTHER PUEBLO INDIAN RESERVATIONS

Generally speaking, visits to the other Indian reservations in
the Southwest are likely to be disappointing. The Zuñi reservation in northwestern New Mexico is in a handsome scenic setting,
and the main community at Zuñi still shows early sandstone
construction, but the impact of modern civilization is apparent,
and one is saddened by the apparent loss of separate identity in
this tribe.

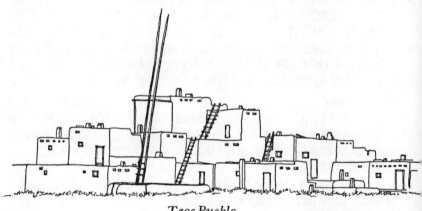

Taos Pueblo

The Rio Grande Pueblo Indians, like the Hopis, do not encourage tourists. The one exception is Taos Pueblo, about 75
miles north of Santa Fe. This pueblo, which was in existence
when the Spaniards first explored the area in 1640, appears much
as it did then, except for the cutting through of windows and

doors. The history of the Spanish attempt to develop good relations with the Indians at Taos is interesting. Colonists came to
the area seeking the fertile lands and plentiful waters of the
region. They were friendly, most of them former Spanish soldiers, and were permitted to set up their homes and farms un-
molested in the immediate vicinity of the pueblo. As the years
went on, the Indians became alarmed at the number of Indian
girls who were marrying the Spanish, and so they politely asked
the Spaniards to move their homes "a league away" from the
pueblo. The Spaniards moved their village as requested, and the
two separate communities have continued down to the present
time. Good relations did not continue indefinitely, however, and
ill will between the Indians and the Spaniards began to develop
late in the seventeenth century, culminating in a bloody Indian
uprising in 1680, which was directed from Taos Pueblo and
which extended throughout the Southwest. In the end, the
Spanish were driven entirely out of the region for a period of
twelve years. Visitors are permitted to enter Taos Pueblo, but
only after paying a fee which, although fair enough, takes a
little away from the feeling of authenticity. The residents look
on visitors with wooden stares, and one does not have any feeling
of welcome. But the pueblo itself is striking.

Detailed descriptions of other Rio Grande Pueblos will be
found in Chapter 6.

THE CONSOLIDATED UTE AGENCY

The Ute reservation is located in southwestern Colorado, not
far from Mesa Verde. A visit here is extremely depressing. The
Ute Indians apparently have been largely swallowed up by modern civilization, and their reservation at Towaoc resembles a
suburban slum, with drab houses spread in all directions, littered
streets, broken windows, and a general air of neglect. It is a sad
sight to see.

Farther north, at Montrose, Colorado, is the Ute Indian Museum, near the center of what was once the great land in which
the Ute Indians roamed freely before they "ceded" it to the

white man in exchange for money and goods. The museum, though small in size, is a happy surprise. It is tastefully and intelligently done, with excellent displays tracing the history, customs, and existence of the Ute Indians from historic times down to the present. Indeed, this museum is a perfect model for the kind of local museum interpreting regional history and customs which should be repeated in other parts of the Southwest but unfortunately is not.

GOOD MANNERS FOR VISITORS

The key to a successful visit to the Indian reservations is to behave as if you were visiting someone's home—which of course you are. A large part of the distrust which can be seen in the eyes of the Indians of the Southwest derives from the behavior of tourists who seem to think they are at a zoo. One should never take photographs of the people, for example, without asking permission. Sometimes a small modeling fee will be requested, which should be paid. Any sign of disrespect, such as laughter or loud talking, should be avoided.

Take care of the land; do not litter or injure plant life.

Dress modestly. Shorts on women, bare feet, dirty hair, and attire which one would not expect to see worn by guests in one's own home should be avoided.

Do not ask prying questions about religious practices or personal beliefs. Respect the right of privacy.

In Pueblo Indian villages it is necessary to locate the governor or other designated representative to determine whether a parking and photography fee is expected. Many pueblos have signs posted limiting the area which visitors may explore. Obey them.

If you are fortunate enough to attend a religious ceremony, show it the same respect you would show in your own church. Dress properly. Behave modestly and quietly. Do not take photographs or make sketches.

Above all, good taste and good manners should be the rule wherever you go. Do not expect the Indians to welcome you with open arms, but do not respond to a cool reception with discourtesy on your own part. Quiet, good behavior will bring many rewards, not the least of which will be the sense that you have not added insult to the injury which so many of our countrymen have already inflicted on these proud peoples.

SHOPPING FOR ARTS AND CRAFTS

In shopping for arts and crafts in the Southwest there are two worthwhile objectives: to find representative examples of the unique Indian cultures of the area and to acquire things for their intrinsic beauty. Above all, one should not approach such shopping with an attitude of "looking for curios," that junk which clutters up the closet back home. The Southwestern Indians produce many objects of remarkable beauty which are well worth having for themselves.

One threshold decision which must be made is to allow enough in your budget to make shopping worthwhile. There are no bargains in the arts and crafts of the Southwest. The things worth buying cost money, usually at least $10 and ranging up to $50 or more for any one item. For that reason, plan your shopping carefully and sensibly and know what you are looking for and why.

Pottery

Among the most intriguing possibilities for collecting in the Southwest are the many different styles of pottery to be found there. And among the satisfactions of this possibility is that much of the pottery made today is in the tradition of pottery made centuries ago, examples of which can be seen in many Southwestern museums. Indian pottery today is still made according to ancient principles. Clay is gathered and pulverized, cleaned to remove lumps and fragments, then wetted down and tempered. The shaping of the pottery is done either by coiling or by modeling and paddling, or by a combination of the two. Once the pot has been shaped, it is dried in the sun and then smoothed down with a scraper. Pots which will be decorated are then covered with slip, sometimes painted on with a rabbit's tail.

Some pots are then polished by rubbing with a small smooth stone. The firing of the pottery is still done by traditional methods, with an open fire covered with natural materials— sometimes damp manure when smudging is desired. After being fired, the pots are wiped and then decorated. This can be done by painting, by carving and engraving, or by impressing designs in the clay before it is fired.

A good program for buying pottery would be to select examples from each of the pueblos that produces its own unique design. Some caution must be exercised, since one or two of the pueblos turn out cheap pottery painted in garish colors purely to satisfy the tourist trade. It is important to look for the designs that are tasteful and traditional. The following list gives a good idea of the range of outstanding pottery currently being made by Pueblo Indians in the Southwest.

Taos Pueblo and *Picuris Pueblo* both make an unpainted pottery which is almost gold in color and glitters with specks of mica.

Cochiti Pueblo produces a cream-colored pottery decorated with designs of plants and birds.

Santa Clara produces polished blackware and redware, on which the polishing marks are evident.

San Ildefonso is the source of the great black pottery developed by Maria and Julian Martínez, with finishes in dull and polished black.

Santo Domingo produces pottery decorated with large birds and plants or geometric patterns on a cream-colored slip background.

San Juan Pueblo produces pottery which is tan with red bands.

Acoma Pueblo produces a thin, hard pottery which is white or tan and decorated with geometric patterns and parrotlike birds.

Zia Pueblo decorates its pottery with a number of varied designs in black, yellow, and red, including stylized birds and animals.

Zuñi pottery has a chalky white slip, with designs painted on it in a brown-black. Zuñi is also well known for its owl figures.

Hopi pottery has bold decorative designs with highly stylized birds, masks, and other shapes.

Baskets

Surprisingly, although baskets played a major role in the early cultural development of the Pueblo Indians of the Southwest, present-day basketmaking is primarily limited to the Hopi Indians. Baskets made with thick soft coils of yucca leaf or grass are woven primarily on Second Mesa. One goal for a collector might be to assemble some of the handsome varied decorations on baskets, which often take the form of almost flat trays and can be mounted on the wall.

Kachina Dolls

The Hopi Indians also are the principal source for kachina dolls, referred to earlier in the section on the Hopis. These dolls, reproductions of the several hundred designs of kachina masks and costumes which are worn by dancers during the first half of the ceremonial year in the Hopi villages, are not playthings but handsome, artistic pieces which are meant to educate Hopi children in the traditions of their people and incidentally provide decoration for Hopi homes. The best dolls, now made for sale as well as for the Hopi people's own use, are carved from the roots of cottonwood trees and tend to be fairly expensive. Dolls can be purchased on the Hopi reservation and also at some of the good museum shops in the Southwest. A number of excellent and varied collections of kachina doll designs have been put together. However, when you have seen one of the large-sized dolls, you will realize that even just one well-made doll can be an important decorative piece, particularly in a modern setting.

Weaving

One of the more ambitious purchases one can make in the Southwest is a Navajo blanket. These items of home weaving, really rugs, represent hundreds of hours of effort by Navajo women to supplement the family income. The Navajos originally wove soft blankets and dresses out of wool raised on their own sheep. When the flocks were destroyed prior to the Long Walk in 1864, the weaving art died out. After their return to the reservation, the Navajos were encouraged to resume the art of weaving but were given new standards to meet in order to satisfy commercial demand. Many Navajo rug designs were actually drawn by traders and copied by the Indians in order to please white customers. Original sketches for some of these early designs can still be seen in the Hubbell Trading Post at Ganado on the Navajo reservation. Despite this evolutionary history, many of the Navajo blankets are extremely handsome and can make dramatic wall hangings in the proper setting. There are specialized designs associated with various sections of the Navajo reservation. Tuba City is the source of a storm-pattern rug featuring lightning designs. Teec Nos Pos produces a rug with geometric shapes outlined in contrasting and frequently brilliant colors. The Shiprock area produces rugs with the traditional elongated figures usually associated with sand paintings. Two Gray Hills features natural wool colors woven in intricate geometric designs, often framed by a black border. The town of Crystal produces a simple design, usually colored with muted vegetable dyes. Wide Ruins-Pine Springs is known for its soft-colored rugs. The Ganado community produces rugs that utilize bold geometric designs with red predominant. Keams Canyon is noted for very large rugs, similar in design to those woven at Ganado.

Silver

Of all the crafts coveted by visitors to the Southwest, silver leads by far. There are three basic design families, reflecting the three major Indian cultures: Navajo, Zuñi, and Hopi. Each culture has produced its own special designs, which are easily recognized after only brief study. Many pieces are extremely handsome and are sought not simply as mementoes of a visit but as beautiful jewelry to be worn and admired.

Working in silver was an early Indian craft, but it received its principal impetus with the arrival of the Spanish. The drive to create silver work on a wide scale, however, did not come until after the Navajo Indians had been resettled following the Long Walk to Fort Sumner after the middle of the nineteenth century. Silver is quite easy to work with. It softens easily with heat and can be beaten into sheets and cut easily. Hammering of sheet silver on a form can produce many shapes for buttons and other decorations. Designs can also be stamped by tapping an iron die into the soft silver. Another technique used extensively by the Navajos is sand casting. For this, molds are carved into sandstone. Molten silver is poured into these molds and, after cooling, bent into the desired configuration.

The most widely known of the Southwest silverwork is that done by the Navajos. Originally, Navajo silver was hammered out of American silver dollars, later Mexican pesos were used, and finally silver blanks were provided by the traders. One of the popular motifs of Navajo silversmiths is the squash blossom, its hollow beads and decorations copied from Spanish pomegranate designs. Squash blossoms are often used together with a crescent pendant, called a *najahe*, believed to have been derived, via the Spanish, from the Moorish design for the pendant charm anciently used on a horse's bridle. The Navajos make many bracelet designs which are extremely popular. They also make handsome belts, buttons, pins, and rings. The patterns of Navajo silver are quite bold and heavy, and many have a Gothic feeling.

The principal characteristic of Zuñi silverwork is the use of turquoise. Silver is used primarily as a setting for large numbers of turquoise stones, often arranged in flowerlike decorative clusters and inlaid and polished so that the surface of the finished piece is completely smooth. Zuñi turquoise and silver bracelets are widely admired among the Indians themselves. The Zuñi silversmiths also make striking necklaces, earrings, and pins.

Hopi silverwork developed after World War II, when a group of ex-servicemen took classes in jewelry making and founded the Hopi Silvercraft Guild under the guidance of Hopi artist Fred Kabote. The Hopi silversmiths use an overlay technique with stylized geometric designs, usually appearing black or dark gray, incorporating traditional Hopi symbolism. Hopi silver has a distinctly modern feeling to it, while still preserving the quality of fine handicraft.

The most important rule when shopping for arts and crafts in the Southwest is to avoid the roadside curio shops. Stores along the major highways with substantial advertising and garish signs generally are places to be avoided if you are looking for quality. Some people shop at trading posts on the reservations, but this takes real experience and an ability to judge quality. There are a number of excellent items, particularly of silver jewelry, at these trading posts, including old "pawn" left by Indians as security for loans on which they have defaulted. By and large, however, the best of these pieces have long since been purchased by collectors, and what remains is not always of first rank, while the pricing is subject to possible inflation.

A much surer way to shop is by going to the cooperative stores established for the express purpose of providing outlets for experienced Indian craftsmen. Among the best of these stores are those located on the Navajo reservation. The Navajo Arts and Crafts Guild was founded in 1941 as a tribal enterprise to promote excellent workmanship and provide better earnings for craftsmen. The main headquarters of the guild are located at Window Rock, and there are well-stocked branches at Tuba City, Navajo National Monument, Monument Valley, Kayenta, Teec Nos Pos, Chinle, and Cameron.

The Hopis have also organized cooperatives where one can shop with confidence: The Hopi Arts and Crafts–Silvercrafts Cooperative, on Second Mesa, and Hopi Enterprises, at New Oraibi.

Also excellent are the gift shops at Bandelier National Monument and at Morfield Village on Mesa Verde.

Many collectors make a point of attending the intertribal ceremonial held each August in Gallup, New Mexico, where some thirty different Indian tribes participate in a presentation of dances, parades, and rodeos and also display for sale a representative variety of their arts and crafts.

PART THREE
Practical Tips and Advice

18
Outfitting Yourself

Experienced campers will scoff at the chapters in this part of the book, but those who have never been on a camping trip will find them useful. One of the great stumbling blocks in planning a trip to the Southwest is concern over logistics. It is one thing to start out on an adventure to see new lands, and it is something else again to get there in relative comfort and safety. The purpose of these chapters is to share as much experience as possible to take away the doubts and worries that face the neophyte.

The first and most important advice of all is this: Do not be timid. Despite all of the seeming obstacles which might cause a sensible person to leave camping to others, it is actually quite easy and enjoyable. The satisfactions of coping for yourself and making do in the open spaces are particularly satisfying to city dwellers, whose ordinary mode of existence is so dependent on others.

To begin at the beginning, the most important item of camping equipment is shelter. Generally speaking this is a matter of taste. Some campers use huge self-contained camping units that resemble buses or moving vans. Others sleep in pup tents. Between these extremes are the various trailers and tents, many of which are relatively inexpensive to rent or purchase. For first-time campers, our advice would be to try a trailer which can be hitched onto the back of your car. There are many collapsible models which are fairly light and maneuverable and yet quite comfortable in the field. The slightly larger enclosed trailers are a shade more comfortable. Either model should do very well for a first experience. If you cannot borrow a trailer from a friend, the chances are that you can rent one fairly easily. Prices obviously vary from place to place, but a family in Illinois can rent a collapsible Starcraft trailer, which will sleep four or five persons comfortably, for approximately $10 a day.

Once you have your camping outfit, the next hurdle is finding suitable campsites. Again, this is much easier than might seem at first blush. The secret is to purchase a copy of the camper's bible, *Woodall's Guide*. A new edition is published each spring and is sold in most bookstores. The 1972 edition sold for $5.95. *Woodall's* contains a section of maps of every state in the United States, as well as Canada and Mexico, with symbols marking communities which have camping facilities nearby. By turning to the alphabetical index of place names arranged by states, one can determine specifically which campgrounds are located near each community marked on the map. This makes finding campgrounds on the road an extremely simple process. *Woodall's* listings include public campsites as well as those that are operated privately. Generally speaking, travelers heading for the Southwest will find that they will probably stay at private commercial campgrounds en route for convenience, since these are generally located near the highway and there is usually no problem finding space quite late into the evening. Commercial campgrounds frequently also provide shower facilities, which are a blessing when you are on the road. One word of warning: *Woodall's* gives the highest ratings to the campgrounds which have the most elaborate facilities, including miniature golf courses and swimming pools. For the traveler who is heading off on vacation with a special goal in mind, these facilities are not likely to be of interest. Because of their high ratings, these campgrounds are often packed and charge comparatively high fees. The optimum campground when you are traveling is one that is located a mile or two away from the main highway so that you do not hear the trucks going by all night long. Peace and quiet, as far as possible, plus clean rest rooms, are really the most important ingredients for satisfactory camping on the road.

When you reach the Southwest, the commercial campgrounds will no longer be appealing, and your goal should be the public campgrounds in the national parks, national monuments, or national forests. Here you will find the camping spaces better separated from each other and the settings often very attractive. Although there are no showers except in the largest facilities, there is usually plenty of running water and a sufficiency of flush toilets. Even the pit toilets in the more remote campgrounds are not as bad as one might think, since they are usually well ventilated and clean. A good rule in picking a campsite in a public campground is to look for the locations on the periphery where you can have an unobstructed view of some of the vistas around you. It is also important to size up your neighbors before you settle in, if you want to avoid those with unleashed dogs, radios, or noisy children. Although it is desirable not to camp too far away from the conveniences, it is also a good idea not to park so close that you are in the line of foot traffic through the evening and morning hours. By following these simple rules you will often find it possible to select camping sites which are completely delightful.

Another bit of advice which you will find most useful is to have one or more gasoline credit cards to use throughout the trip. Particularly when you have the extra load of a trailer to haul, gasoline is consumed at a very high rate on a cross-country trip and in climbing up and down mesas and mountains. If you buy all of your gas for cash, you will find that you have spent as much as $200 or $300, which means that you will have to cash traveler's checks or worry about having sufficient funds to buy groceries and other things along the way. Although the credit card does not save you any money, it does save you aggravation and worry. In the Southwest, the gas stations one finds most frequently are Phillips 66, Chevron (Standard Oil), Texaco, and Shell (Conoco). It would be a good idea to have credit cards from at least two of these companies with you. One other word of advice: Never let your gas tank get too low. It is surprising how many long stretches of road there are in the Southwest with no gas stations at all. It is not unusual to find a 60- or 70-mile stretch without even a house. A wise traveler follows the rule of having his gas tank filled whenever it reaches the halfway mark.

The basic camping setup should include a place to sleep, a place to cook, and a place to clean up. Campgrounds generally provide picnic tables and fireplaces at each campsite, plus access to toilets and running water. The rest is up to you. Most campers have their own bedrolls, which are warm and comfortable and mighty welcome at the end of a day of exploration. Unless you have a built-in mattress in your camping unit, it is also a good idea to bring along an air mattress to cushion the hard surface beneath you. The only other sleeping equipment you may want is a pillow plus pillow case, which will give you a special touch of extra comfort.

There are many excellent portable camp stoves on the market. Despite the apprehensions of those who have not tried them, the Coleman stoves are remarkably efficient and safe. Coleman fuel is available at most food stores and large campgrounds anywhere in the country. It is a mistake to rely solely on wood fires at campgrounds as a source of cooking heat, since many campgrounds prohibit collecting firewood.

A good lantern is also an important piece of camping equipment. Flashlights and battery-operated lanterns are useful additions, but nothing can beat a gas-operated lantern, which throws a wide ring of bright light, to eat a late supper by. Again, the Coleman products are as good as any.

Another important convenience is a supply of two or three hard rubber or plastic washbasins, plus a plastic wastebasket, if you are traveling by trailer. These can be purchased in most large variety stores. Part of the camping ritual is washing dishes after breakfast and supper, using water that has been heated over the Coleman stove. This becomes an art, since the supply of hot water is limited. A shallow washbasin is the perfect tool for doing the job well. Such a washbasin is also desirable for shaving and washing one's face and hands. The other basic items of equipment which should not be forgotten are: your driver's license and registration; an emergency gas can *filled* with gasoline; and a telephone credit card (if you'll need to call home). Another important item is a plastic water jug, preferably the 2½-gallon size, which can be comfortably carried from a water spigot some distance away from your campsite and yet provide sufficient water to prepare a meal and wash the dishes.

In addition to the utensils needed for cooking (listed in the next chapter), here is a check list of useful items which should be included on most automobile camping trips, subject to personal preferences and interests:

Folding chairs—the aluminum kind with plastic webbing are fine —to provide some comfort in the evenings after a long day's drive.

Cameras and film (take plenty).

Postcard address list and stamps.

Writing equipment, for letters, notes, shopping lists.

Guitar, if you play one (but, please, no transistor radios unless you *must* have one—in which case play it very softly).

Sketching equipment; drawings or paintings will bring back memories when you get back home.

Metal folding table, extremely useful for your cooking and dishwashing chores.

Tool kit; something always seems to need repairing.

Masking tape, Scotch tape, and white glue, to mend things.

Wooden matches.

Playing cards and other games.

Rubber bands, to hold together folders and maps, which pile up.

Knapsack, for picnic lunches on the trail and for carrying rock specimens back to camp.

Scissors and string.

Shaving mirror.

Canteen; never head off on a hike in the Southwest without a canteen full of water.

Clothespins and a length of clothesline; even if you do not do any hand laundry, you will want to dry out clothes after a rain.

Thermos bottle with plastic lining, or plastic juice container, for lemonade or iced tea on luncheon picnics.

Plastic tablecloth, to make campground picnic tables more attractive.

Small tray; particularly if you have a trailer, a tray can save countless trips back and forth bringing out breakfast and supper things.

Laundry bag.

Insect repellent, although it is surprising how few insects there are in the Southwest.

First-aid kit, and it is not a bad idea to take along a snakebite kit as well, available in many drugstores.

Alarm clock.

Those who are heading off on their first camping trip will probably make the mistake of taking along too many clothes. Obviously this is an area where personal habits and tastes control, but a list for a four-week camping trip to the Southwest is offered as a starting point. Bear in mind that there are wide ranges in climate, from hot desert temperatures to quite frigid mountain air. Also bear in mind that the habit of a daily bath and a clean change of clothes is a luxury which is not essential to human existence. On the camping trail, one shower and one trip to a laundromat in a week is about average.

Here is a suggested packing list for the women in the family:

1 pair of sneakers
1 pair of hiking boots
1 pair of sandals
2 pairs of long pants plus a belt
4 or 5 shirts
2 pairs of shorts
1 wash-and-wear dress
1 cotton skirt
2 pairs of hiking socks
1 week's supply of underwear
1 bathing suit
1 bath towel and washcloth
1 wool sweater
1 windbreaker or hooded sweatshirt

1 light sweater
1 raincoat
1 sun hat
1 light nightgown
1 pair of flannel pajamas
  Overnight case

The following is a comparable packing list for the men:

2 pairs of trousers (khaki is excellent)
4 shirts
1 pair of sneakers
1 pair of hiking boots
2 pairs of hiking socks
1 pair of loafers or moccasins
2 pairs of socks
4 changes of underwear
1 pair of swimming trunks
1 bath towel and washcloth
4 handkerchiefs
1 pair of heavy cotton pajamas
1 belt
1 heavy sweater
1 windbreaker
1 raincoat
1 sun hat
1 jacket and necktie
  Shaving kit

Clothing for children is essentially the same, subject only to their ages and special requirements.

Soft baskets or canvas bags are excellent for stowing clothes. Suitcases can be very clumsy. Rolling your clothes and packing them end up in your bag saves packing space and makes each item easy to find.

One final word. With more and more people enjoying the parks, they will become less and less enjoyable unless each of us leaves a clean campsite. It is most unpleasant to arrive at a beautiful spot at the end of the day only to find that its last occupants have left the ground littered with aluminum pop tops, cereal box covers, and other reminders that you are not the first person to enjoy the place. Clean up thoroughly before you leave, and deposit your trash in the container put there for the purpose. If there is no container, carry your trash with you until you find one.

19
Food and Drink

You will be surprised at the changes in your appetite when you are on a camping trip. Food becomes one of the most significant parts of the day's activities. Breakfast is a much more important meal than you can imagine. The time available to spend on food preparation is limited and must be used wisely. When you have only one burner to work with, food preparation is also a challenge. The limited number of dishes available also·affects planning. Even trips to the supermarket on the road take on a special new significance and meaning. Every member of the family participates in decisions on what to buy.

Family favorites and personal tastes obviously will govern your own meal planning, but there are some basic concepts worth knowing so that you do not make the mistake of loading up with the wrong things and finding that your first meals are disasters.

When you are out in the open all day you will find that you crave a substantial breakfast. Bottled fruit juice is a good way to start the day. You will find, in addition, that fresh fruit is appealing to the appetite. Particularly in summertime, melons, fresh peaches, whole oranges, and bananas are good things to serve at breakfast. Cereal is also a breakfast staple. In the desert climate cold cereals are perfectly acceptable, but you will be surprised at how good hot cereal tastes out of doors, especially in the higher altitudes. A number of instant hot cereals are available in most supermarkets, packaged in individual envelopes which are just right for making a single bowl. By adding hot water from the camp stove, a delicious dish of steaming hot cereal is ready for eating. When you do not have to break camp to move on to another location, the additional touch of eggs with bacon or corned beef hash makes breakfast a true luxury. Because of the problem of cleaning pans, soft-boiled eggs are often more convenient than any other form. Instant coffee and milk are, of course, regular items on the breakfast menu.

When you are traveling on the road, or off exploring on a trail trip, lunch is a welcome break in the day, but you will not want to spend much time over it. Generally speaking, sandwiches are the answer, together with lemonade or iced tea, and maybe cookies or grapes and a candy bar for dessert. Some sandwiches which can be put together easily on a camping trip will be obvious to any homemaker, including those that start with a base of cream cheese or peanut butter. Where a few extra minutes can be spent, taking the time to chop up some celery and mix it with mayonnaise and canned tuna fish or shrimp can make lunch a special occasion.

The evening meal is obviously the most important one of the day when you are out camping. Contrary to one's ordinary expectations, the best camp dinner is not steak or hamburgers over a charcoal fire, which is usually too messy, too time-consuming, or too complicated. The key to successful suppers is the one-dish meal. This involves dumping various ingredients into a single pot which can be heated over a one-burner stove. A stew made with fresh hamburger meat, canned chicken, or canned tuna is always successful. One can add various ingredients, such as canned vegetables, minute rice, and tomato sauce. Sloppy Joes, made from hamburger meat and a sauce mix which is packaged in foil envelopes and is available in most supermarkets, also go well at a campsite. Another good, and quick, meal is canned beef stew combined with a can of roast beef in gravy to increase the meat content. A relatively new item on the market is the Hunt's Skillet Dinner, which is a kit containing all the ingredients for a one-dish main course, to which you must add one pound of ground beef. There are at least six different ones currently available—from Stroganoff to lasagna—and they are very good.

These one-dish meals are usually supplemented with snacks beforehand if one is in the habit of having a cocktail before dinner. Celery and carrot sticks are particularly tasty with a Russian dressing dip. For some reason, the crisp, juicy texture (and perhaps the vitamin content) of these raw vegetables fills a special appetite need when you are living outdoors. Nuts, chips, and dips also help fill the stomach. Generally speaking, dessert is not called for, as everyone usually heads quite quickly for bed or to the campfire talk.

A number of good camp cookbooks have been published, and one or two of them on your travel bookshelf will help inspire variety in your meals.

A word about beverages is in order. It is surprising how dependent you become upon water, and how much time you spend looking for sources of water along your way. The first rule of thumb is to fill your water tank, utility jug, and canteens every chance you get. Drinking water is available at most campgrounds. Some even have elaborate rigs for filling up trailer water tanks. Water can also be obtained in most gas stations if you fail to get a supply when you break camp. The important thing to remember is to try to keep all of your water containers filled at all times. You will also find that hot water is a precious commodity. First thing every morning, and first thing when you set up camp, some member of the group should put a kettle full of water on the stove and start it heating. Hot water is essential, not only for cooking but also for shaving, washing faces and hands, and doing the dishes.

Most campers drink far fewer sweet carbonated beverages than one would imagine; these are not terribly thirst-quenching in the Southwest. Far more satisfactory are the instant iced tea mixes which come in premeasured envelopes complete with sugar and lemon flavoring, so that all you have to do is pour them into a container of water and ice. They are sold in most super-markets. Lemonade is also good for variety.

Ice, incidentally, is one of the most precious commodities of all on a camping trip. Most ice chests are designed to take block ice, which is an item that Americans long used to refrigerators have forgotten. There are few things more satisfying than chopping with an ice pick into a large block of ice which yields pieces of clear, clean ice for a cool drink.

A cocktail at the end of the day can be one of the great pleasures of a camping trip for those so-minded, but too much alcohol is bad news. Generally speaking it is wise to avoid any alcoholic drink at noontime, even beer. The climate and fresh air take a heavy toll, and the simpler nonalcoholic beverages like iced tea and lemonade are far more refreshing. Even those who are accustomed to drinking beer or wine with dinner will find that their capacity for alcohol is sharply reduced in the desert or at high altitudes. One or two drinks before dinner tend to be about all one can handle without unfortunate aftereffects. If you do count on an evening cocktail, be sure that you have an adequate supply of liquor with you. Some states in the Southwest sell liquor only in state stores which are open for limited hours each day. On the Indian reservations, it is impossible to buy any liquor at all.

Here are some useful check lists for planning your cooking and eating needs:

COOKING UTENSILS

1 teakettle
1 moderately large pan with cover for stews
1 frying pan
1 small pan for boiling eggs
1 bowl for salads
2 sharp knives
1 cooking spatula
1 large cooking spoon
1 large slotted spoon
1 large cooking fork

1 can opener
1 vegetable scraper
1 rubber spatula

EATING UTENSILS (For a Family of Four)

4 bowls (plastic rather than metal, which draws off heat)
4 luncheon-size plates (ditto)
4 coffee cups (ditto)
5 forks
5 dessert spoons
5 teaspoons (the extra fork and spoons will prove useful in cooking and serving
4 knives
4 plastic tumblers
5 oz. paper cups
9 oz. paper cups

DRINK-MAKING GEAR

1 ice pick
1 beer can opener
  Beverage mixes
2-quart plastic juice shaker (for mixing iced tea, lemonade, etc.)

MISCELLANEOUS SUPPLIES

Dishwashing liquid
Paper towels
Paper napkins
Toilet tissue
Soap and soap dish
Pot scrubber
Sponges
Dish towels
Kleenex

In picking out the utensils and equipment to take with you on your camping trip, be sure that you select your favorite knives, bowls, pots, and the like. It is extremely important to have equipment you can work with effectively and easily. Do not feel the need to load yourself down with every conceivable item you might use, since you are not going to Outer Mongolia. There are stores everywhere in the Southwest where you can buy items that have been forgotten.

Above all, take along your best disposition and spirit of ad-venture. You will encounter some minor crises and calamities along the way, but if you greet them with patience and good humor they will only add to the over-all enjoyment that will make your trip to the Southwest one of the greatest experiences of your lifetime.

20
Notes for the Noncamper

Although camping out of doors is unquestionably the best way to see the Southwest, it is not the only way. Camping has the advantage of permitting full enjoyment of sunsets, stars, and sunrises, in the setting of rocks and canyons. But for those who prefer to travel with less equipment, or closer to inside plumbing, it is still possible to see a lot of the Southwest by automobile, staying at motels and lodges.

One obvious way to visit the Southwest is to fly to one of the major cities, rent a car, and visit some of the outstanding sights, ending up in another Southwestern city to fly home. This approach makes it possible to savor much of the atmosphere and feeling of the Southwest in two weeks or less. For the purpose of flying to the Southwest and renting a car, the most convenient starting and stopping points are Albuquerque, New Mexico; Phoenix or Tucson, Arizona; Las Vegas, Nevada; Salt Lake City, Utah; and Denver, Colorado. All these cities are within a half day's drive of the Colorado Plateau, with the exception of Denver, which involves driving through the Rockies and requires an extra day of travel for most motorists but is well worth it. Each of these cities has attractions of its own which might justify spending some time there as well, but not at the expense of a good visit to the Southwest.

Albuquerque is New Mexico's largest city. Founded in 1706, the original plaza still exists with its feeling of early history and Spanish traditions. The handsome University of New Mexico is here, with various exhibit buildings concentrating on the Southwest. Nearby are a number of pueblo ruins and early missions. Also nearby is Santa Fe, founded in 1609 and the oldest state capital in the nation. The adobe Palace of the Governors dates from before the arrival of colonists on the East Coast and faces on the old plaza, which was the terminus of the Santa Fe Trail, the major trading route between the territory and St. Louis. Although somewhat spoiled by tourism, there is still much of the old town to be seen, including San Miguel, said to be the oldest church in the United States. Among the special sights are the units of the Museum of New Mexico with exhibits on Indian life and culture.

Phoenix is a large industrial and resort center with a climate that attracts many people for health reasons. The city is located in the middle of the Arizona desert, surrounded by irrigated fruit and vegetable farms. Among the unusual features is the Desert Botanical Garden, featuring cacti and other plants indigenous to the desert climate; the Heard Museum of Anthropology and Primitive Arts, with a collection of 400 kachina dolls; and the Arizona Mineral Museum, with specimens of minerals, ores, and gems.

Tucson is also a desert city with a resort flavor. The University of Arizona campus includes important collections of art and artifacts, as well as pioneer history and minerology. Nearby Tucson Mountain Park features desert and mountain scenery and the Arizona-Sonora Desert Museum of animals and plants, which includes a tunnel gallery of underground animal lairs, plus a Western movie set of "Old Tucson."

Las Vegas likes to think of itself as an entertainment center but is really a string of gambling casinos in a setting of gaudy hotels, neon lights, and floor shows, fascinating for those who like that sort of thing but completely out of key with the natural beauty of the Southwest. Originally settled by the Mormons in

1855, it failed as a mining town, then turned to ranching before the arrival of the railroad in 1905 began the modern era.

Salt Lake City is exciting in both its setting and its origins. The city continues to stand as a tribute to the courage and fortitude of the Mormon pioneers, who overcame unbelievable adversities to build their own community in the middle of the desert. A visit to the Temple Square is thought-provoking in its demonstration of the power that religion can have in the modern setting. A drive down Emigration Canyon to the spot where Brigham Young said "This is the place" is spine-tingling. The campus of the University of Utah is well worth seeing, and the Great Salt Lake, although insect-ridden, is a wonder of nature that deserves a visit once in a lifetime.

Denver owes its birth to gold and silver prospectors but today is a typical large modern city. Its sights include the Denver Art Museum and the Colorado State Museum, with dioramas and other exhibits depicting the history of the early West. Unusual places to visit include the gold display at the United States Mint and the handsome Air Force Academy at Colorado Springs.

Packing lists obviously have to be modified to include clothing for travel by air and arrival in a city setting. For the purpose of visiting the Colorado Plateau, basic clothing of the type previously described should be brought along.

Decisions on where to stay overnight obviously will be affected by your own travel schedule and timetable, but the following list of accommodations is offered to help you plan your visits to the special sights described in this book. This is a basic listing only, and anyone seeking more complete information should refer to up-to-date listings or current travel guides, such as those published by the Mobil Oil Corporation and usually available for purchase in Mobil gas stations, as well as many bookshops. The Mobil Travel Guides are revised annually, and new editions are usually available in the month of April. Two separate editions are necessary to cover the Colorado Plateau: *California and the West* (which includes Arizona and Utah) and *Southwest and South Central Area* (which includes Colorado and New Mexico). The Mobil Travel Guides are published by

Simon and Schuster, 630 Fifth Avenue, New York, N.Y. 10020.

For those who prefer to reserve accommodations through a chain, the following motels could be used as bases for automobile excursions into the Southwest country. It should be understood, of course, that much of the flavor and feeling of staying on the site is not available to those who limit themselves to stereotyped commercial lodging, although it is still possible to see and enjoy the scenery.

RAMADA INNS

Albuquerque, N.M.
Gallup, N.M.
Santa Fe, N.M.
Cortez, Colo.
Flagstaff, Ariz.
Moab, Utah

TRAVELODGES

Albuquerque, N.M.
Farmington, N.M.
Gallup, N.M.
Santa Fe, N.M.
Durango, Colo.
Flagstaff, Ariz.
Winslow, Ariz.
Cedar City, Utah
Moab, Utah

HOLIDAY INNS

Albuquerque, N.M.
Farmington, N.M.
Gallup, N.M.
Santa Fe, N.M.
Durango, Colo.
Flagstaff, Ariz.
Kayenta, Ariz.

Arches National Park, Canyonlands National Park, Dead Horse Point State Park

There are no overnight accommodations in any of these three areas, except for campgrounds. All three, however, can be easily visited using Moab, Utah, as a base. In fact, the possible side trips from Moab are so good that it is worth thinking in terms of spending two or three nights there while visiting the various nearby sights. Arches National Park is only 5 miles northwest on U.S. 160. Dead Horse Point State Park is a longer trip (12 miles north on U.S. 160, then 22 miles southwest on the side road) but perfectly feasible for a day trip. There are several roads into Canyonlands National Park from Moab, and it is best to visit the park headquarters, which is located right in the city of Moab, to learn about road conditions and to plan your trip. In addition to these three principal sights, there are spectacular views along the scenic river route along the Colorado River, just north of town. A number of boat trips and guided tours are also available.

Moab has half a dozen commercial motels, the best of which are: The Green Well, 105 South Main Street, Moab, Utah 84532 (801-259-6151); Moab TraveLodge, 550 South Main Street, Moab, Utah 84532 (801-259-6171); and Ramada Inn, 182 South Main Street, Moab, Utah 84532 (801-253-9741).

Bandelier National Monument

Bandelier can be visited from Santa Fe, New Mexico, which is 46 miles away, but for full enjoyment one should try to stay at the Frijoles Canyon Lodge, which is located right in Bandelier next to the visitor center. The lodge has a snack bar and provides overnight accommodations in cabins. Accommodations are rustic and not luxurious, but they are perfectly in keeping with the flavor and spirit of the park area. The address is Frijoles Canyon Lodge, Los Alamos, N.M. 87544 (505-672-3655).

Canyon de Chelly National Monument

There is an unusually nice lodge located right in the Canyon de Chelly National Monument, adjoining the campground and not far from the saddle-horse stable. The lodge is small, but it has air-conditioned rooms, a good cafeteria, and is well run. The address is Justin's Thunderbird Lodge, Box 548, Chinle, Ariz. 86503 (602-674-5443). There is also a motel in Chinle itself not far from the monument entrance: Canyon de Chelly Motel, Box 295, Chinle, Ariz. 86502 (602-674-5288). Special Jeep tours into the canyons can be arranged at Justin's Thunderbird Lodge.

Capitol Reef National Park

Accommodations at Capitol Reef National Park are sparse but well worth the special effort because the park itself is so spectacular. There is a small lodge within the park, located just ¾ mile from the visitor center, which is quite simple and basic but perfectly adequate: Capitol Reef Lodge, Torrey, Utah 84775 (801-425-3558). There is also a small motel 8 miles west of the visitor center on State 24: Rim Rock Motel, Torrey, Utah 84775 (801-425-3843).

Great Sand Dunes National Monument

There are no overnight accommodations at Great Sand Dunes National Monument except for the campgrounds. This means the noncamper can visit the monument only in the course of a through trip, and since the distances are substantial from other sights, it may well be that a visit to Great Sand Dunes National Monument is not worth the effort unless one is planning to be in this area anyway. The great fun of the monument is staying overnight in the campground and watching the long shadows of sunset and sunrise moving across the dunes.

Mesa Verde National Park

Mesa Verde National Park is blessed with superb motel accommodations right in the heart of the park and very convenient to the ruins. The view is spectacular and the cafeteria is good. The address is Far View Motor Lodge, % Reservations Manager, Mesa Verde Company, Box 277, Mancos, Colo. 81328 (303-529-4421). A brand-new restaurant features traditional Indian foods. There is also an economy family cabin court, Point Lookout Lodge, at the entrance to the park, and a number of motels at Cortez, 10 miles west of the park entrance.

Zion National Park

Zion also has a lodge located right in the heart of the park itself, with excellent views and comfortable accommodations.

Zion Lodge is operated under a concession from the Department of the Interior and provides a number of rooms in cabins in a style and setting compatible with the spirit of a visit to a national park. In addition to a restaurant and a good shop, the lodge has a swimming pool (open to all for a modest fee) which provides a refreshing change at the end of a hot day. The address is: Zion Lodge, Springdale, Utah 84767 (801-772-3213). There are also several motels in the town of Springdale, just outside the southern entrance to the park, the best of which are: Driftwood Lodge, Box 98, Springdale, Utah 84767 (801-772-3262); and Pioneer Lodge, Box 116, Springdale, Utah 84767 (801-772-3233).

The Indian Reservations

The outstanding place to stay in the Indian country is the new motel adjoining the Hopi Cultural Center on Second Mesa in the heart of the Hopi reservation. The address is: Hopi Cultural Center Motel, Box 67, Second Mesa, Ariz. 86043 (602-734-2401). This is a very comfortable modern motel, handsomely designed and appointed, with a good café restaurant. The perfect combination for a good visit to the Indian reservations would be to spend one night at the Hopi Motel on Second Mesa and another night at Justin's Thunderbird Lodge at Canyon de Chelly (see above). There is also a motel at one of the eastern entrances to the Navajo reservation, at Window Rock, the headquarters of the Navajo tribe: Window Rock Motor Inn, Box 706, Window Rock, Ariz. 86515 (602-871-4108); and a Holiday Inn at Kayenta, Ariz. 86033, near Navajo National Monument and Monument Valley (602-697-3221).

All of these accommodations are reported to be good places to stay, and some of them are spectacular. As a result, there are times when the demand for rooms far exceeds the supply. To avoid disappointment, therefore, it is urgently recommended that reservations be made as far in advance as possible, and that deposits be sent on to assure that the reservations will be honored.

Index

245

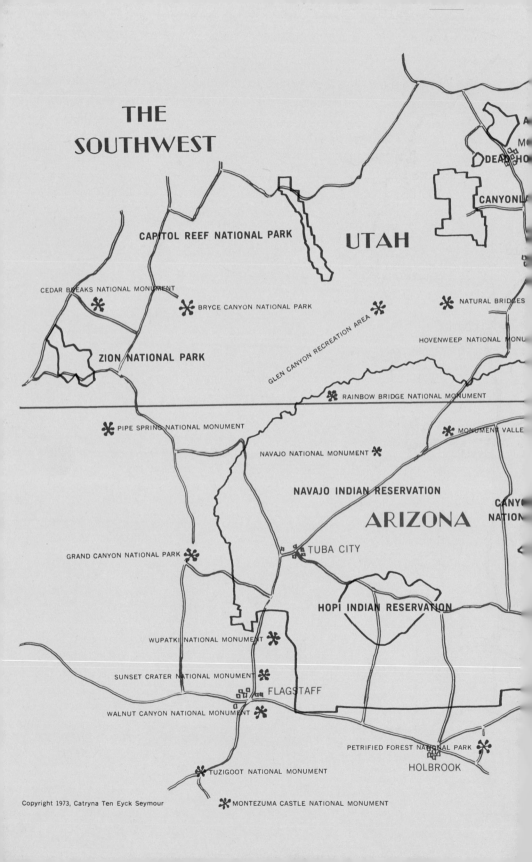

THE
SOUTHWEST

CAPITOL REEF NATIONAL PARK

UTAH

DEAD HO

CANYONL

A
M

CANYONLA

CEDAR BREAKS NATIONAL MONUMENT

BRYCE CANYON NATIONAL PARK

NATURAL BRIDGES

HOVENWEEP NATIONAL MONU

ZION NATIONAL PARK

GLEN CANYON RECREATION AREA

RAINBOW BRIDGE NATIONAL MONUMENT

PIPE SPRING NATIONAL MONUMENT

MONUMENT VALLE

NAVAJO NATIONAL MONUMENT

NAVAJO INDIAN RESERVATION

ARIZONA

CANY
NATION

GRAND CANYON NATIONAL PARK

TUBA CITY

HOPI INDIAN RESERVATION

WUPATKI NATIONAL MONUMENT

SUNSET CRATER NATIONAL MONUMENT

FLAGSTAFF

WALNUT CANYON NATIONAL MONUMENT

PETRIFIED FOREST NATIONAL PARK

HOLBROOK

TUZIGOOT NATIONAL MONUMENT

MONTEZUMA CASTLE NATIONAL MONUMENT